LIVING
BEYOND THE FRAME

LIVING
BEYOND THE FRAME

by Cheryl J. Harris

CREATION
HOUSE
A STRANG COMPANY

LIVING BEYOND THE FRAME by Cheryl J. Harris
Published by Creation House
A Strang Company
600 Rinehart Road
Lake Mary, Florida 32746
www.creationhouse.com

Unless otherwise noted, all Scripture quotations are from the Holy Bible: New International Version. Copyright © 1973, 1978, 1984, International Bible Society. Used by permission.

Scripture quotations marked MSG are from *The Message: The Bible in Contemporary English*, copyright © 1993, 1994, 1995, 1996, 2000, 2001, 2002. Used by permission of NavPress Publishing Group.

Author photo courtesy of Alavekios Photographic Essays, Woodinville, WA

Cover design by Mark Labbe

Library of Congress Control Number: 2006926079
International Standard Book Number: 1-59979-010-6

First Edition

06 07 08 09 10 — 987654321
Printed in the United States of America

To my parents, Vernon and Joan Crockett: like the Mona Lisa, you are the "real thing" and have lived your lives with so much integrity. Much of you is in this book.

To Harlan: because every day you have modeled for our girls and me a life being lived beyond the frame.

To Cheylan and Taryn: my prayer is that you will both know how much God loves you and that you will let Him reveal the masterpiece He has created in you.

Acknowledgments

THANK YOU TO...

Jesus: for drawing me to You at the beginning, and for bringing me back every time I wandered away. The words on these pages are not worth reading if You are not in them.

Harlan: it blesses me daily that you love God more than anyone. Thank you for encouraging me to listen to His voice and to be obedient to His calling. I cannot count the number of times you were holding down the fort while I was teaching this material. You are truly someone who knows how to lay down his life for others. Thank you.

Ted Cannon: thank you for the challenge of reading through the Chronological Bible in one year. Boy, was I mad at you! But I began to hear God in new ways because of that challenge, and this book began there.

Monica Alvarez: you were inviting people to my house to hear lessons that had not been written yet. Now *that* is faith. Truly, there would be no book if you had not plunged ahead in the midst of my resistance. Your belief in me and enthusiasm for the material has made all the difference. Thank you.

The First Class: the guinea pigs—Crystal, Katie, Monica, Eileen, Becky, Diane, Amy, Angie, Dawn, Kathy, Debbie, and Linda. Thank you for enduring that first year and contributing so much to the exercise content of the final draft. Your openness to let God use the material and your willingness to share the results has been inspiring.

Frank and Betsey Hernandez: it is a God story that I love to tell—a bump in the hallway, a "chance" meeting with an old friend, and an introduction to a publisher, all in three short days. Thank you for being so generous with your contacts and your words of encouragement.

Strang and Creation House: thanks to David Welday for hearing something in the unprepared pitch worth reading. Allen Quain for reading it and taking a chance on it. Virginia Maxwell for always answering the phone and all of my questions. Sandra Clifton and Elaine Caggiano for their editing prowess and encouraging comments. Mark Labbe for a very clever cover.

Jesus, the First and the Last: thank You for blessing these beginnings. Whatever becomes of the rest is in Your hands for Your glory!

Contents

Preface

WHENEVER SOMEONE ASKS me how this book came to be written, I struggle with the answer. I never intended or desired to write a book. Its existence is as much a surprise to me as to anyone else. As in all things in my life, it has as much to do with what others have done as it does with anything I have.

In December 1998, a close friend challenged me to read through the chronological Bible in one year. I didn't want to. I was not terribly interested in the Old Testament and felt that God came across as harsh and unforgiving in those stories. But I was also someone who couldn't resist a good challenge, especially from that friend in particular.

That year now seems like a miracle year; one of God revealing to me all the places He had been present in my life that I had overlooked. I am now in my sixth year of reading through the Bible, and God continues to reveal new things, new insights, and new understanding of His incredible mercy and provision, both in those old stories and in my life.

I began to write down some of the lessons I was learning in short story format and another friend read them. She was so encouraged by them that she began to invite people to my house for a Bible study, insisting that I should teach what I had learned. I have observed after teaching it and facilitating discussions about the content that nothing much has changed between Moses' time and today. People everywhere have been given a dream or vision by God, but many people are immobilized by their own belief that there is something about them or their past that disqualifies them from accomplishing it.

The purpose of this material is to help the reader see the truth about who God is and who they are in relationship to Him, to enable them to realize and live in their new identity in Christ, to release them from the prison of fear that immobilizes them, and to help them remember all that God has done in their lives. The reader will be able to see their lives from God's perspective and therefore be released by His power and presence into a life worth "living beyond the frame."

CHAPTER 1

A Picture Worth a Thousand Frames

T AKE A LOOK at the picture below. What is it?

One of the world's most famous works of art is Leonardo da Vinci's *Mona Lisa*. For centuries we have been captivated by the masterpiece and have reproduced its image on everything from posters to postcards. The original, however, hangs in its frame in the Louvre. The frame of this masterpiece protects and enhances the work of art, but is worth very little in comparison to the painting. The frame supports the masterpiece, but it is not the masterpiece itself.

THE PURPOSE OF THE FRAME

As valuable as the *Mona Lisa* is, our lives, created by a loving Father, are even more valuable. We are His masterpiece, His work of art:

> For we are God's workmanship, created in Christ Jesus to do good works, which God prepared in advance for us to do.
> —EPHESIANS 2:10

The question, then, is what is the frame? The frame is the structure that surrounds our lives. The structure takes on several forms, much like the roles we play in our lives. For instance, I am a spouse, parent, child, sibling, grandchild, friend, colleague, boss, employee, and student. I have a certain type of heritage and live in a particular environment. I have peculiar characteristics, behaviors, and skills. I hold to certain beliefs.

There are also labels that I carry with me. Some of them are ones placed on me by other people, and others are labels I have placed on myself. Whatever they are, or wherever they came from, labels make up part of what frames us. When the roles or labels are positive and in correct proportion, they can give our lives structure and purpose.

The difficulty comes when we focus the majority of our time, money, and efforts on maintaining the frame, rather than discovering the beauty of the masterpiece within it. It is not that everything about the frame is bad, but our focus on it can be misplaced. If the frame becomes too big in our perspective, it can hide God's purpose, power, and plan for our lives. Like the picture on the first page, the picture can be obscured when the frame is too large. Let's look at the same picture from a wider perspective. Can you guess what the whole picture contains?

Granted, it is not much, but you are probably getting a better idea of what is in the rest of the picture. Right now the frame is still huge in comparison to the picture.

The purpose of this book is to begin looking at our lives from God's perspective. He is able to see the whole picture, the entire beautiful work of His hand. In order for us to see ourselves in the way in which He sees us, we need to carefully remove what blocks our vision so that we can see more...

More of what God sees...
More of what He intended...
More of His purpose....
More of His power...
More of His presence....
More of His grace...
More of His amazing love...

And more of what makes our lives the Masterpiece of His creation.

LIVING BEYOND EXERCISE

1. Make a list of all roles or labels that you feel have described you in the past, or that currently describe you. You may want to get a pad of sticky notes and write one item per note. These individual notes will be used again in the next chapter.

2. Locate at least one passage of Scripture that supports the concept of living beyond the frame.

3. Find a person—Biblical, historical, or current—who lives beyond labels or expected roles and inspires you to do the same. An example might be Helen Keller, who, though blind and deaf, became a teacher and author.

4. Arts and crafts time: draw a picture that represents your life as God's masterpiece. Draw a frame around that picture that, in size, represents your current focus on it. Try not to judge yourself on this part. Just be honest with yourself.

5. Meditate on Ephesians 2:10 and Psalm 139. Ask God to show you a picture of how He sees and loves you.

CHAPTER 2

How People Change

I THINK PEOPLE SPEND an inordinate amount of time and money on books and seminars dealing with self-help, or even "Christ-help" formulas for kicking bad habits, living a more fruitful life, or developing ministry. My experience is generally positive with those investments, but they always fall short of real breakthroughs. Sometimes I feel that although I "know" what the outcome is supposed to look like, I fail to achieve it or endure the process long enough to see any real or lasting results.

It is kind of a long story, but for several years I taught a couple of classes a week on weight management for a particular organization. I am not sure who learned more during those years, but I discovered that often when learning a lesson in God's Word, His answers would come to me in a seemingly unrelated topic while teaching or preparing to teach my classes. God uses everything, I am convinced.

One day while I was teaching the weight management course, I used a pyramid chart that portrayed a progression of change. I had taught on this chart many times, and had seen the chart posted on the wall many more times than that. The chart is actually not necessarily a weight management progression, but originally comes from language acquisition studies. It demonstrates how humans experience change, as when learning a new language, attempting to break a habit, or in this particular case, reducing one's weight.

Pyramid of Change

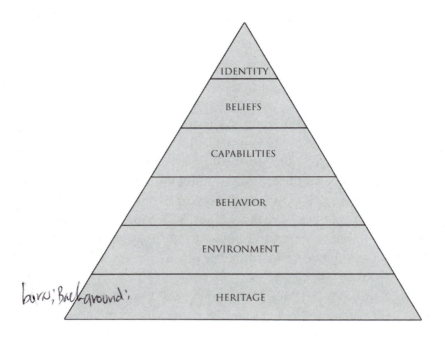

Perhaps a short explanation will help.

The easiest way to learn to speak French is to be born to French-speaking parents and be raised in France (or for purposes of a later illustration, French-speaking Switzerland). This is obviously the foundation of the pyramid. Unfortunately, none of us can exercise any control in this matter. We either were or were not born in France. If we are not already French, some action on our part must take place in order to learn the French language. The remaining levels of the pyramid will assume that I did not receive the French heritage or its language.

The next best way to learn a new language is to move to the country where the language is spoken, therefore you must first move to France. This illustrates a change in environment. With that move, your method of communicating your needs immediately changes. Let's assume the first immediate need is to find a bathroom. Instead of just asking for a bathroom, you may engage in a little game of charades to get your message across to any person who looks remotely helpful in your new environment (you are not in Kansas anymore!) This demonstrates a change in behavior. After all, people probably would not tolerate this embarrassing display if you were back at home . . . at least not for long after discovering that you actually do know how to ask for a bathroom in your native tongue. But when in a different country, people can be sympathetic to a person who needs help but does not speak the native language. Someone will eventually offer to teach you the phrase in French so that you no longer have to play charades to meet this most basic of needs. You have now moved up the chart to capabilities. You are capable of getting yourself to a bathroom without much public humiliation (another great incentive for affecting change in one's life: avoiding embarrassment).

Pretty soon you get better and more efficient at getting your message across using language about your need for a bathroom. It may be the only sentence you know in French, but at least you know it. This displays an increase in Capabilities. After awhile, you have the bathroom question down and begin to believe that you have the ability to learn other phrases in French. After all, if you can learn that first important question of where the bathroom is located, you begin to believe that you can learn other sentences. With each additional phrase learned and each successful event of being shown the bathroom instead of a banana, your faith or Belief increases. Each skill builds on the other and your belief in yourself grows larger.

This process repeats continuously, and eventually you may begin to "identify" more with the French culture and language than with your native tongue. Could a person actually acquire a new identity through this method of change? Could you imagine yourself being French rather than your own nationality? This actually occurs to people who have resided for long periods of time in a country other than their origin. I know of such a person.

A TALE OF TWO SISTERS

I met Katie when she was in her early forties. A relative of my husband, she had come with her husband to visit her sister, Ann, in Southern California. Katie had lived the last twenty years in the part of Switzerland that spoke only French (now you understand my previous reference). But Katie moved there when she was only nineteen years old. It was amazing to watch her interact with her sister. Imagine, there was Ann conversing with no recognizable accent (both of us being from the west coast of the United States). Katie, however, was trying to interpret for her French-speaking husband and fumbling with the meaning of certain English words. Katie's accent was almost as thick as her husband's.

I was so intrigued by this phenomenon that I asked Katie if she still felt like an American, or did she feel more Swiss? She indicated that it had been many years since she felt like she belonged to her culture of origin and actually reminisced about the exact moment she realized that she no longer felt American. She shared the story.

It was the morning (after living there for many years) that she awoke with the realization that she had dreamed in French. Whoa! I had never even thought of that. Katie and I were both born in the United States, but Katie dreamed in French and I dreamed in English. How could that actually happen? It was amazing. Katie's transformation had been so complete that I could not imagine her ever sounding like her sister Ann. She dressed differently. Her mannerisms were different. Everything about Katie was different from Ann, except her genetics. She had completely changed her identity. She was not just someone who happened to know how to speak French, she was a French-speaking Swiss!

Katie's experience is a perfect example of how a person can change her environment, which changes her behavior, which changes her capabilities, which changes her beliefs, which ultimately changes her identity. Katie, through this process and over many years, became a very different person than she would have been had she remained in the United States.

LIVING BEYOND EXERCISE

1. Using the sticky notes from the previous lesson, identify which level of the pyramid best describes each "label" or "role." For example, if the label is "great cook," the level that best describes that note may be capabilities. Another note may fall into several areas of the pyramid, depending upon the person. For instance, the label of "Christian" may describe behavior or beliefs to some and identity to others.

2. After placing each label in its category, determine which category seems to be the biggest barrier to your own progress. Again, this is very personal and subjective. The category on which you choose to focus may or may not be the category with the most number of sticky notes on it. Try not to judge yourself and be as honest as possible.

3. Pray and meditate on this category. Ask God to reveal whatever He desires in relation to that category.

4. Find a passage of Scripture or character study in God's Word that reveals God's power over that category.

CHAPTER 3

How God Changes People

I WAS TEACHING THE process of change and using the pyramid of change in my weight management class one morning. I was directing attention to the chart and making my point about how a person experiences change as a series of progressions through the stages of the pyramid. If you want to lose weight, you must first change the environment (remove all the "bad foods" from your house), which will begin to change your behavior (by snacking on the good food that is left in your house), which will begin to build confidence in your capabilities (to choose good food over bad food), which will begin to change what you believe about yourself (I can always make better choices) and eventually change your identity (I am a healthy person who knows how to choose good food). In the middle of my explanation I heard God say to my heart, *Not so with Me.*

Now, I do not hear the voice of God quite so clearly every day and certainly the venue of a weight management class was unusual. Not wanting to be derailed from my stream of conversation, I continued, kind of placing God on hold, because I was not sure I had really heard Him. God said again, *Not so with Me.* The message was clearer and much louder, a voice that I could not ignore. I paused long enough to silently ask God to let me finish with my class. I promised Him that I would return to the conversation.

I finished my point and concluded my class in the allotted time, even though the subtle nagging continued. I needed to take up the topic with God when I could concentrate on what He might be trying to say to me. As I was driving home I asked God what He wanted to tell me. He said, "Flip the chart over…that is what I give you." I went home and drew the chart out the normal way in my notebook and then drew it with the labels in reverse. Identity was now at the bottom wide part and heritage was located at the top.

This seemed to make sense. Of course, God was saying that His identity was the foundation of it all. We are changed, called children of God, while we were yet sinners and we are a new creation. This was great! I got it. I was quite pleased with myself and put my notebook away for another day.

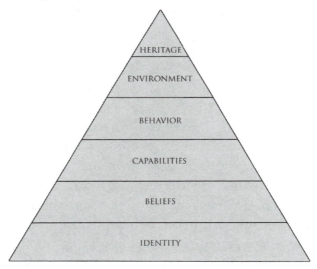

Unfortunately my satisfaction was short-lived. The feeling that I did not have it quite right continued to nag me. Although it seemed right to have identity as the foundation of God's change pyramid, my diagram did not feel completely right. I struggled with this for a couple of days, praying and attempting to listen more closely to God and how the original chart, in reverse, related to Him.

After several days I was looking at both charts, side by side, and realized that it indeed was only partially right. I could not put my mental finger on why, but decided to let go of my pride and start again with the original chart. I tried to remember what God had said to me that day as I was driving home from class. He had asked me to flip over the chart. That is all. Is that what I did? Not exactly! I flipped the labels' positions on the chart, but that was not what He had asked me to do. I grabbed my little notebook again, but instead of drawing out the second pyramid as I had done before, I just flipped the original chart manually. It was then that I saw my error.

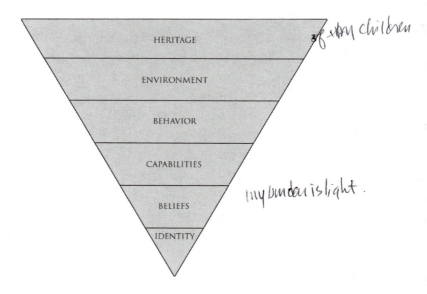

God had asked me to flip the chart, not the labels! At the time, this difference did not seem like such a big deal; a small difference really. Why did it bug me so much? I decided to just go with it. So, on my third try I ended up with the original pyramid so that the labels were in the same place, but the point of the pyramid was on the bottom.

So novel is this idea of an upside-down pyramid, I could not even find a template for it on any software. The pre-programmed pyramid could not even be flipped over but had to be redrawn from scratch. In other words, we just do not think this way in everyday life!

I still did not know the impact of this seemingly small detail until much later, so I will keep you in suspense for a little while longer. Hopefully, it will all make sense eventually.

Now, regardless of point down or wide part down, identity is truly the source of all change found in Christ. Not many Christians would dispute this assertion. I believe that what God was trying to say, however, is that the process of change in Him is exactly the opposite of what we have come to know as "normal" in every other part of our lives. So normal, in fact, that most of us do not realize that we are going through this process when trying to change a simple habit or learn a language, for example. Only when it is pointed out does someone say, "Oh yeah, that is exactly what happens." Although the original pyramid of change is normal in our human nature, an altered life in Christ, rather than flowing out of a new environment, flows from a change in identity...namely, the identity of Christ.

The crux, then, is that God gives us His identity (you are a new creation, while "we were yet sinners"). It is His identity and how closely we relate to it and experience it in daily living that makes a change in what we believe, both about Him and about ourselves.

So now let's try the process of change in reverse. It is His identity that through increased faith begins to alter that of which we are capable. It is His identity, through increased faith and new ability that begins to alter our everyday behavior over time. Finally, it is His identity and association with Him that ultimately affects and changes our environment and impacts our world. Increased faith, improved skills (like sharing our faith), better choices, and ultimately impacting our world (engaging in ministry) are the supernatural results of identifying with Christ.

All of these levels, flowing from the source of identifying with Christ, are seen as areas of struggle for today's Christian (and yesterday's too). When the original pyramid of change is applied to the Christian life, that life can become burdensome, troublesome, offensive, legalistic, and unrelatable to the world to which we are called to give the good news. What does that look like?

Let's say that I am not yet a Christian. I get up enough courage to come to a church service, hoping a change in environment will somehow change my circumstances or me. I meet a couple of nice people and start to come regularly. I soon realize that there is an implied expectation that I will cease some of my "worldly" behaviors. I have found that some of my old behaviors are easy to leave behind, but there are others that are more difficult. I become secretive about those old patterns and feel bad that I am not strong enough to overcome them. Someone invites me to help out in one of the ministries of the church, but I know that I am not qualified because of those bad behaviors that still linger. Eventually I become frustrated with myself because I cannot seem to sustain positive change in certain areas and I realize that my faith is not strong enough and I will never truly belong. The guilt is too much. Over time I lose heart and return to my old life, never fully becoming connected in the church or qualified to be there.

Have you ever known anyone like this? Have you ever been someone like this?

And God says again, *Not so with Me!* Using God's way brings relief. It is what is meant in Matthew 11:28:

> Come to me, all you who are weary and burdened, and I will give you rest.

Jesus' own words broke through the trap of the original pyramid and released us from the responsibility of making our own way through change, with our own resources. The gravity and weight of the original pyramid is lifted.

One result, for the many of us who sometimes feel disqualified in ministry due to our own shortcomings, is the freedom from trying to "figure it all out." We do not need to desire or chase after ministry. Ministry is the supernatural outcome of repetitive presence of God because of His identity. Exposure to it is like the exposure of raw camera film to light—it changes the outcome and the image. What a relief! I am not required to change behavior or "get good" at something or be super-spiritual or find just the right ministry. What He asks is for us to be *intimate* with Him, exposed to His light, so that our image (beliefs, capabilities, behavior, environment, and heritage) is changed. Come to His throne and rest in Him. The rest comes—supernaturally.

It seems that wherever I go, I run into fellow Christians who feel that they have been given a particular vision or mission for their lives, but they experience frustration at the seeming lack of progress toward that God-given picture. They feel stuck within the borders of their life's frame: lack of education or ability, current familial and financial obligations, or a feeling of disqualification because they know, all too well, their own weaknesses. They feel imprisoned by the original pyramid.

Remember the French lessons? In essence, God has done for us in an instant what only years in a new environment could do for Katie. Imagine yourself as a freshman struggling through your first year of studying French, on the eve of a major examination. You are cramming, trying to remember syntax and verb tense, and sweating the whole ordeal over a late-night pizza. You try to sleep, but the stress of tomorrow's required performance keeps you from any real rest.

Now, you awaken the next morning and suddenly realize that God has transformed you into a native of France. You are on your way to your exam, remember, the one for which you were cramming last night. Are you worried about syntax and verb tense of the French language today? No way! The examination is going to be a snap, because yesterday you were a college student with no experience and little knowledge of the language, but today *you are French!* (I am thinking there might be more than a few students in their first year of language study who pray for this miracle of miracles on a fairly regular basis).

You not only speak French fluently, you feel French, you dress French, and all of your life experiences are of France. Tonight you will even dream in French! What a gift for someone in his first year of language study, to be given the gift of the French *identity*. Wow!

That is what it is like with God. Now read the following two passages of Scripture in light of the French lesson:

> So from now on we regard no one from a worldly point of view. Though we once regarded Christ in this way, we do so no longer. Therefore, if anyone is in Christ, he is a new creation; the old has gone, the new has come! All this is from God, who reconciled us to himself through Christ and gave us the ministry of reconciliation: that God was reconciling the world to himself in Christ, not counting men's sins against them. And he has committed to us the message of reconciliation.
> —2 CORINTHIANS 5:16–19

21

For this reason, since the day we heard about you, we have not stopped praying for you and asking God to fill you with the knowledge of his will through all spiritual wisdom and understanding. And we pray this in order that you may live a life worthy of the Lord and may please him in every way: bearing fruit in every good work, growing in the knowledge of God, being strengthened with all power according to his glorious might so that you may have great endurance and patience, and joyfully giving thanks to the Father, who has qualified you to share in the inheritance of the saints in the kingdom of light. For he has rescued us from the dominion of darkness and brought us into the kingdom of the Son he loves, in whom we have redemption, the forgiveness of sins.

—COLOSSIANS 1:9–14

The ability to identify with Jesus and what He did on our behalf is the source, the impetus, the conduit through which all other changes and effective ministries occur. To believe that anything from our own hands can be eternal, we must always start and finish there.

LIVING BEYOND EXERCISE

1. Meditate on the 2 Corinthians and Colossians passages. Are there other passages that illustrate the power of the flipped pyramid and God's identity as the source of change?

2. If you believe that you have received a vision or life mission from God, describe it and any Scripture passages that have helped confirm it.

3. The "Big Fat Question": remembering that everything flows from God's identity in us, if you knew that you could not fail or disqualify yourself from your life's mission, what would you be doing right now? What would be your next step? Has God been trying to move you in a direction or has He asked you to do something? Are you hesitating? If so, why?

CHAPTER 4

The Fear Factor

MANY YEARS AGO, (I do not remember when), I heard the word *fear* used as an acronym for: False Evidence Appearing Real.

★★★★★★★★★★★★

I once read a fable about a man traveling on a road toward an important destination. While on his journey he came upon a very large, very angry-looking bull in the middle of the road. In fact, the snorting bull was blocking his path. There was no way to get past the bull and still stay on the road. The road was bordered by thick jungle.

The traveler had a choice to make. He could turn back and forget about getting to his destination, he could get off the road and try to go around the bull by going through the jungle, or he could face the bull. After much time passed and all options were weighed, the traveler decided to face his fear of the bull. The destination was too important to leave behind and its call too strong to be delayed by the jungle. So, in the midst of his fear, he walked straight toward the bull and grabbed it by the horns (yes, I believe this is where the expression comes from).

To his amazement the bull did not attack him, but instead, began to speak. "It's about time you came. I have been waiting for you. Climb on my back and I will take you to where you are going."

✶✶✶✶✶✶✶✶✶✶✶✶

Of course, the moral of the story is that many times the very thing we fear is the thing that, if confronted, will propel us toward our greatest reward or success. In the story, the bull only looked menacing and angry. The reality is that facing our fears, whatever they may be, can be the vehicle that transports us to our destination, to the vision that God has put in our hearts.

THE BIG FAT QUESTION REVISITED

In all of our lives, there is The Big Fat Question that seems to loom larger and larger as the months and years of our lives pass. If God has placed a calling in our lives, and we always seem to be looking in the other direction, what is keeping us from turning around and running toward the vision? We may answer the question from the last chapter's exercise differently. The details of the answer may be as varied as the people who answer it, but if we feel like our spiritual "feet" are cemented in place there is generally the same root problem. We are afraid. We fear that something on that pyramid of our lives disqualifies us from being used by God. Although we know in our minds that God's power and love can overcome, somehow we just feel that our weakness is too great. If you could identify that thing you fear most about fulfilling God's calling on your life, what would it be? Return to the last chapter's Big Fat Question and try to capture the answer in one word, a word that describes a fear or something that you feel may disqualify you. Write the word below:

FEAR of: _____

Remember the flipped pyramid? Write your "fear" word in the category where you think it best fits. Three people may end up using the same word but place it in different categories of the pyramid. For example, let's use the word *failure*. Failure for one person may fit best under capabilities, because he feels that he is being called into an area where he currently has few skills. A biblical example of this would be Solomon, who was unsure of his capabilities of leading God's people. Someone else may share your fear word for failure, but might place that word under the behavior category. Moses might have felt disqualified, due to the fact that he had murdered an Egyptian. Certainly, God could not overlook that behavior! Someone else may put failure under heritage because they have a family history that does not seem promising. Remember all those people who said, "Does anything good come from Nazareth?" Apparently even a poor heritage is not enough to overcome the will and power of God. Whatever your word is, write it in the category that you feel best fits your situation and briefly describe in the margin why the category fits your fear word.

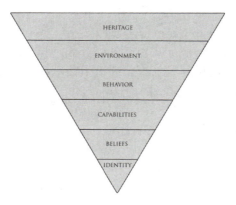

Different Fears, Same God

In today's world, we have a special name for just about every kind of fear. I looked it up. There are approximately 530 different phobias. I am not talking about those types of fears. I am talking about the type of fear that prohibits a person who hears the call of God in their heart to move their spiritual legs. There is a bull in the road. There is something that causes us to check every move, question every decision, and spiritually immobilizes us. Something appears real, but in God's perspective it is only a lie.

Another Life Lesson

If I were to perform the above exercise, I would have to place my fear somewhere between the *capabilities* and *beliefs* categories. What sometimes immobilizes me is the fear that someday I will forget how good God is and forget that all blessings come from Him. You remember King Solomon? Somehow, at the end of his life, he forgot everything that God had done. He suffered from spiritual amnesia, and outlived his faith in God. Although I experience fear in other ways, this fear is the one that can immobilize me and cause me to question myself to the point that it leads me in wrong directions.

My fear of what I might do wrong and its affect on my life's course can be illustrated in the events of a recent outing on a friend's boat. We had spent a beautiful day out on the lake watching the kids being pulled on inner tubes and relaxing in the sun and the breeze created by the speed of the boat. When evening came it was time to return home. That is where the lesson began.

My friend's teenage son was driving the boat. Although he is young, he is becoming quite a good boat driver. He began to experience some difficulty, however, when he entered the channel in the lake that requires all boats to slow down to five miles per hour. He was having significant difficulty keeping the boat straight and headed into the channel. Back and forth we wove in the channel as the teenager attempted to correct and re-correct his way through. It actually became a bit annoying for all of the passengers. So annoying was the weaving, in fact, that his dad began to instruct him from the back of the boat to keep the boat straight. Although the instruction was well-intentioned, it was probably not helpful.

At the same time, I, who had a little boat-driving experience myself, as well as an aptitude for teaching, wanted so badly to help out the struggling teenager. Surely I could give him some helpful and more specific instruction to aid him in keeping the boat straight in the channel. Immediately, I felt God's check on my heart—and mouth. My boat wisdom was not to be shared at this time. I was frustrated. So much advice to give and yet God was telling me to keep quiet. I came to the conclusion that God must want the teenager to learn the lesson in some other way.

Finally, we were through the channel and our young driver could finally throw the throttle forward and resume our trip across the lake. It did not take me long to realize that the weaving was no longer noticeable. He was still moving the steering wheel as much as he was at the slower speed, but now the corrections were hardly perceptible. I sat across from him and marveled at the difference. And then it hit me.

The lesson was not for the young man. The lesson was for me! How often I am seasick from all of the corrections and over-corrections that I conduct throughout my day. I weave back and forth, and the weaving is obvious because I am moving so slowly. My spiritual eyes are focused right on my bow, right where my feet are walking and no further down the path!

I am glad I chose to listen to God that day and keep my instructions to myself. If I had chosen to be the teacher that day, I would have missed the opportunity of being God's student!

How many times does God ask you to trust in Him, to take your eyes off the bow, and look out across the horizon? How often does God ask you to leave your worries, your reserve, and your fears behind—and just floor it? The spirit is willing, but the flesh is weak!

LIVING BEYOND EXERCISE

1. Below is a wheel that represents an average human lifespan. With the arrow being the starting point, mark this with a "0" or your date of birth. Then count clockwise and label any major event of your life where it should be on the wheel, each line representing one year of your life. For instance, I was baptized when I was eleven years old, so on the eleventh line I would place a dot, or star, and then label the margin "baptized." Some other events to label might be:

High school graduation

College graduation

First job

Marriage

Birth of child

Wheel of Life

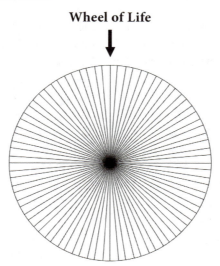

2. Read and meditate on the Scripture passage on the next page.

ISAIAH 51

"Listen to me, you who pursue righteousness and who seek the LORD : Look to the rock from which you were cut and to the quarry from which you were hewn; look to Abraham, your father, and to Sarah, who gave you birth. When I called him he was but one, and I blessed him and made him many. The LORD will surely comfort Zion and will look with compassion on all her ruins; he will make her deserts like Eden, her wastelands like the garden of the LORD. Joy and gladness will be found in her, thanksgiving and the sound of singing. "Listen to me, my people; hear me, my nation: The law will go out from me; my justice will become a light to the nations. My righteousness draws near speedily, my salvation is on the way, and my arm will bring justice to the nations. The islands will look to me and wait in hope for my arm. Lift up your eyes to the heavens, look at the earth beneath; the heavens will vanish like smoke, the earth will wear out like a garment and its inhabitants die like flies. But my salvation will last forever, my righteousness will never fail. "Hear me, you who know what is right, you people who have my law in your hearts: Do not fear the reproach of men or be terrified by their insults. For the moth will eat them up like a garment; the worm will devour them like wool. But my righteousness will last forever, my salvation through all generations." Awake, awake! Clothe yourself with strength, O arm of the LORD; awake, as in days gone by, as in generations of old. Was it not you who cut Rahab to pieces, who pierced that monster through? Was it not you who dried up the sea, the waters of the great deep, who made a road in the depths of the sea so that the redeemed might cross over? The ransomed of the LORD will return. They will enter Zion with singing; everlasting joy will crown their heads. Gladness and joy will overtake them, and sorrow and sighing will flee away. "I, even I, am he who comforts you. Who are you that you fear mortal men, the sons of men, who are but grass, that you forget the LORD your Maker, who stretched out the heavens and laid the foundations of the earth, that you live in constant terror every day because of the wrath of the oppressor, who is bent on destruction? For where is the wrath of the oppressor? The cowering prisoners will soon be set free; they will not die in their dungeon, nor will they lack bread. For I am the LORD your God, who churns up the sea so that its waves roar—the LORD Almighty is his name. I have put my words in your mouth and covered you with the shadow of my hand—I who set the heavens in place, who laid the foundations of the earth, and who say to Zion, 'You are my people.'" Awake, awake! Rise up, O Jerusalem, you who have drunk from the hand of the LORD the cup of his wrath, you who have drained to its dregs the goblet that makes men stagger. Of all the sons she bore there was none to guide her; of all the sons she reared there was none to take her by the hand. These double calamities have come upon you—who can comfort you?—ruin and destruction, famine and sword—who can console you? Your sons have fainted; they lie at the head of every street, like antelope caught in a net. They are filled with the wrath of the LORD and the rebuke of your God. Therefore hear this, you afflicted one, made drunk, but not with wine. This is what your Sovereign LORD says, your God, who defends his people: "See, I have taken out of your hand the cup that made you stagger; from that cup, the goblet of my wrath, you will never drink again. I will put it into the hands of your tormentors, who said to you, 'Fall prostrate that we may walk over you.' And you made your back like the ground, like a street to be walked over."

CHAPTER 5

Walking Through Fear

MY DAD IS quite a funny guy. When he reached the age of sixty he began to joke about it. He would say, "You know, the average lifespan for a man is only about seventy or eighty years. If I'm lucky I'll reach eighty, which means I'm now already three quarters of the way there. Now that may not seem like a big deal, but I'll tell you, when I'm driving around in my car and look down and see that I only have a quarter tank left, I start nervously looking around for the next gas station!"

If my dad were to color in the used portion of the Wheel of Life from the previous chapter's assignment, it would look like this:

DAD'S WHEEL OF LIFE

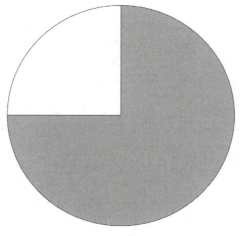

Without being too morbid, this visual representation illustrates the necessity to move beyond whatever fear exists that holds us back from God's purpose. Regardless of how much of our wheel has been used up, there are no guarantees that any of us will be allotted eighty years. There are no "somedays" or "later when I'm ready" options. As Paul admonishes the church in Corinth:

> As God's fellow workers we urge you not to receive God's grace in vain. For he says, "In the time of my favor I heard you, and in the day of salvation I helped you." I tell you, now is the time of God's favor, now is the day of salvation.
> —2 CORINTHIANS 6:1–2

Truly then, knowing the Savior and experiencing His grace without fulfilling His purpose in us is "in vain." Allowing fear to hold us back is contrary to His will. Think of the 2 Corinthians passage from the unsaved point of view rather than the saved. It is easy to get confused about what Paul writes until you read the passage that immediately precedes it. It is Paul's discussion on the ministry of reconciliation:

> Since, then, we know what it is to fear the Lord, we try to persuade men. What we are is plain to God, and I hope it is also plain to your conscience. We are not trying to commend ourselves to you again, but are giving you an opportunity to take pride in us, so that you can answer those who take pride in what is seen rather than in what is in the heart. If we are out of our mind, it is for the sake of God; if we are in our right mind, it is for you. For Christ's love compels us, because we are convinced that one died for all, and therefore all died. And he died for all, that those who live should no longer live for themselves but for him who died for them and was

raised again. So from now on we regard no one from a worldly point of view. Though we once regarded Christ in this way, we do so no longer. Therefore, if anyone is in Christ, he is a new creation; the old has gone, the new has come! All this is from God, who reconciled us to himself through Christ and gave us the ministry of reconciliation: that God was reconciling the world to himself in Christ, not counting men's sins against them. And he has committed to us the message of reconciliation. We are therefore Christ's ambassadors, as though God were making his appeal through us. We implore you on Christ's behalf: Be reconciled to God. God made him who had no sin to be sin for us, so that in him we might become the righteousness of God.

—2 CORINTHIANS 5:11–21

If we are to be in the business of reconciliation, we must fully recognize that we are new, ourselves. It is difficult to bring good news of being new to another person without first experiencing its reality ourselves. Whatever fears held us back prior to God reconciling us, we must now move beyond them. Because of God's grace, He has provided us with an incredible example.

A CLOSER LOOK AT MOSES

If you were raised in a Christian home or have been a Christian for any length of time, you may feel that you know the life of Moses intimately. For the sake of everyone else, a little refresher course may be in order.

Moses was the little baby placed in a floating basket by his mother, a scheme to save his life when the Pharaoh at the time was choosing to exercise his power over the Hebrew slaves by killing all of the male children born to that nation. He was drawn out of the water by Pharaoh's daughter and lived his

37

entire childhood and young adult life as the grandson of Pharaoh. All of his needs were provided for and he received the best education that was available in Egypt at that time. This was definitely not a bad lifestyle.

Then things got complicated. As an adult he witnessed an Egyptian beat one of the Israelites, the people of his heritage, and took matters into his own hands by killing the Egyptian. It wasn't until the next day that he discovered that other Israelites were aware of this act and did not appreciate his interference. To make matters worse, Pharaoh was not thrilled either and attempted to kill Moses. What did our future brave leader do? He ran. He saved himself and ran away in fear—to Midian, in the Sinai Peninsula.

He met a priest of Midian who offered his daughter Zipporah to the "Egyptian" who helped her draw water from a well. For the next forty years Moses tended to his father-in-law's flocks. Moses raised a family and continued to enjoy a peaceful life, successfully escaping his punishment in Egypt. There is no Biblical evidence that he ever attempted to return to Egypt for forty years. When Moses ran from his fears, it was for good! And then it all changed, because God Himself intervened.

> Now Moses was tending the flock of Jethro his father-in-law, the priest of Midian, and he led the flock to the far side of the desert and came to Horeb, the mountain of God. There the angel of the LORD appeared to him in flames of fire from within a bush. Moses saw that though the bush was on fire it did not burn up. So Moses thought, "I will go over and see this strange sight—why the bush does not burn up." When the LORD saw that he had gone over to look, God called to him from within the bush, "Moses! Moses!" And Moses said, "Here I am." "Do not come any closer," God said. "Take off your sandals, for the place where

you are standing is holy ground." Then he said, "I am the God of your father, the God of Abraham, the God of Isaac and the God of Jacob." At this, Moses hid his face, because he was afraid to look at God. The LORD said, "I have indeed seen the misery of my people in Egypt. I have heard them crying out because of their slave drivers, and I am concerned about their suffering. So I have come down to rescue them from the hand of the Egyptians and to bring them up out of that land into a good and spacious land, a land flowing with milk and honey—the home of the Canaanites, Hittites, Amorites, Perizzites, Hivites and Jebusites. And now the cry of the Israelites has reached me, and I have seen the way the Egyptians are oppressing them. So now, go. I am sending you to Pharaoh to bring my people the Israelites out of Egypt."

—EXODUS 3:1–10

Ten verses spill out of the Old Testament, like water from a glass. It is not a long passage when one considers that it changed the course of Moses' life and the course of human history. It is amazing. God has heard the cries of His people and in response is sending them—wait for it—an eighty-year-old man who has done nothing for the last forty years except walk around the Sinai Desert with a bunch of sheep. And he only started that profession after turning his back on his very privileged upbringing and forty years of luxury by murdering an Egyptian. No wonder Moses responded to the call the way he did.

But Moses said to God, "Who am I, that I should go to Pharaoh and bring the Israelites out of Egypt?"

—EXODUS 3:11

Moses knew exactly who he was. The frame of his life made him completely unsuitable for any kind of service, especially the release of God's people. Can you see Moses' labels on sticky notes—murderer, criminal, fugitive, loner, and sheepherder? Worst of all, maybe one of the labels was "Non-Israelite."

Remember the last interaction he had with them? The Israelites knew that Moses had killed the Egyptian but they did not trust him. With a temper like that, he might lash out at the slaves next. And he was no longer on speaking terms with Pharaoh's family, either. That one act of murder had placed Moses in a sort of "no-man's-land." He was no longer the adopted grandson of Pharaoh and not accepted by his blood relations, the Israelites. Yes, Moses knew exactly who he was, and who he was not. He was not a person who should be considered for this type of work or mission. He was a murderer and a coward. And God responded to Moses, assuring that He would be present:

> And God said, "I will be with you. And this will be the sign to you that it is I who have sent you: When you have brought the people out of Egypt, you will worship God on this mountain."
>
> —EXODUS 3:12

Isn't it interesting that God's sign to Moses will be evident only *after* he has been obedient? His promise is that the whole nation will meet God on the same mountain where Moses now stands staring into the burning bush. The mountain is called Mount Horeb, which is also called Mount Sinai.

Now let's take a look at what Moses' Wheel of Life would look like at this point. First of all, we have to remember that the life expectancy was longer, and we just happen to know in hindsight how many years were allotted to Moses (a significant advantage over what we can see in our own Wheel of Life). The wheel represents the 120 years of Moses' entire life.

So Moses spent forty years in the palace of Pharaoh learning how to govern, and the next forty years in the Sinai learning how to live in the wilderness. It does not appear to be an impressive resume. Years in the desert as a shepherd had to look like a demotion from his bright beginnings in Pharaoh's house. No doubt, Moses was being groomed for leadership throughout the first forty years of his life. The next forty years, however, were far less eventful, at least in Moses' eyes. But God knew that both parts of those eighty years were needed in Moses' training if he were to lead the Israelites out of Egypt and prepare them for the desert life that stood between them and God's promise.

Moses's Wheel of Life

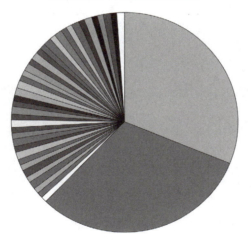

A LITTLE IRONY

Only God could have orchestrated such a plan. The life-changing event for Moses was the day he witnessed the Egyptian beating one of the Israelite slaves. His response to that encounter altered his life's path, but not forever. Had things gone differently, he might have been considered a hero for defending the slave. One could describe his actions as heroic; he could have been called a savior of the defenseless! Isn't that what we might have called him if he lived in today's world? Think of it. A royal son stops an oppressor in his tracks.

Under his own strength and will, Moses failed miserably at being the savior of even one Israelite slave. But now God had used the lessons of the last eighty years to transform this headstrong murderer into a humble servant. This time, under God's protection and will, Moses would become the savior of a nation of slaves. Although hesitant at first, Moses was faithful to obey. By the time the Israelites were getting their feet dusty on the Red Sea floor, he was confident of his leadership and mission.

LIVING BEYOND EXERCISE

1. Take another look at your Wheel of Life. Are there
areas of events on the wheel that you feel "disqualify"
you from service? Are there events that are missing from the wheel because you think they are too
shameful to mention? Remember, God was able to
use Moses' shameful actions to move him toward
new things. Look at the Wheel again and add those
things that you may have omitted as being beyond
God's reach for usefulness.

2. In the previous chapter's exercise, you were asked
to meditate on Isaiah 51. Are there any portions of
that passage that affected or touched you? List the
passage and your response to it.

CHAPTER 6

Fear and the Wilderness Journey

BEFORE WE CONTINUE with the transformation of Moses, let's review the journey of the Israelites and their difficulty in following his leadership. Their feet had not even touched the Red Sea floor when the Israelites began their complaining. Out of earshot of Egypt's Pharaoh and the tyranny of generations of slavery,[1] another tyranny took over—the tyranny of the unknown. At every opportunity their newly earned freedom was compared with the "comforts" of the life they had known. You name it, they complained about it:

Safety

> As Pharaoh approached, the Israelites looked up, and there were the Egyptians, marching after them. They were terrified and cried out to the LORD. They said to Moses, "Was it because there were no graves in Egypt that you brought us to the desert to die? What have you done to us by bringing us out of Egypt? Didn't we say to you in Egypt, 'Leave us alone; let us serve the Egyptians'? It would have been better for us to serve the Egyptians than to die in the desert!"
> —EXODUS 14:10–12

Water

> Then Moses led Israel from the Red Sea and they went into the Desert of Shur. For three days they traveled in the desert without finding water. When they came to Marah, they could not drink its water because it was

bitter. (That is why the place is called Marah.) So the people grumbled against Moses, saying, "What are we to drink?"

—Exodus 15:22–24

Food

In the desert the whole community grumbled against Moses and Aaron. The Israelites said to them, "If only we had died by the Lord's hand in Egypt! There we sat around pots of meat and ate all the food we wanted, but you have brought us out into this desert to starve this entire assembly to death."

—Exodus 16:2–3

More Water

The whole Israelite community set out from the Desert of Sin, traveling from place to place as the Lord commanded. They camped at Rephidim, but there was no water for the people to drink. So they quarreled with Moses and said, "Give us water to drink." Moses replied, "Why do you quarrel with me? Why do you put the Lord to the test?" But the people were thirsty for water there, and they grumbled against Moses. They said, "Why did you bring us up out of Egypt to make us and our children and livestock die of thirst?"

—Exodus 17:1–3

Leadership

When the people saw that Moses was so long in coming down from the mountain, they gathered around Aaron and said, "Come, make us gods who will go before us. As for this fellow Moses who brought us up out of Egypt, we don't know what has happened to him."

—Exodus 32:1

It is difficult to conceive that a people condemned to slavery for generations would view freedom as a worse situation, but the uncertainty of wilderness living continually had the Israelites turning their heads and wishing for the safety of the familiar. And the constant complaint was the same, "Why did you bring us up out of Egypt? We're going to die out here!" At every turn their worst fear was that they would die in the desert. Whether the cause was lack of food, lack of water, or lack of safety, the desert was going to get them and in the end the fault landed at the feet of Moses. In their view, it would be better to be slaves in Egypt than continue to follow him and end up as corpses in the wilderness.

And God responded. Where there was bitter water, He made it sweet. When there was no food, He provided quail and manna. When there was no water available at all, He provided it out of a rock. And when the people grew bored from Moses' absence on Mount Sinai, God showed mercy. He also showed them the difference between a powerless idol created out of earthly goods, and the power of the living God who changed a bunch of slaves into a free nation overnight.

He was also in the process of transforming these same former slaves into warriors who would conquer their enemies and take hold of the land God had promised them. After nearly two years of their complaining and all of God's provision and constant presence, they finally reached their destination.

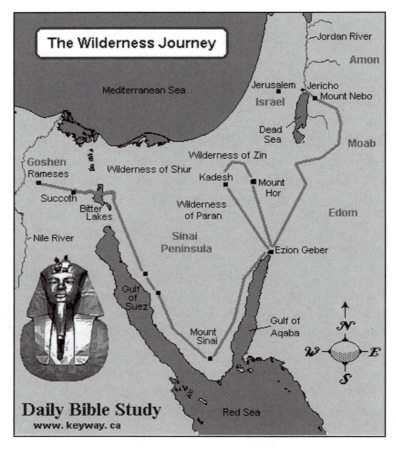

The Wilderness Journey

Jordan River

Amon

Mediterranean Sea

Jerusalem Jericho

Israel Mount Nebo

Dead
Sea

Moab

Goshen Wilderness of Zin
Rameses Wilderness of Shur

Kadesh

Wilderness of Zin

Mount
Hor

Succoth

Bitter
Lakes

Wilderness
of Paran

Edom

Nile River

Sinai
Peninsula

Ezion Geber

Gulf
of
Suez

Gulf of
Aqaba

N

Mount
Sinai

W   E

Daily Bible Study
www. keyway. ca

Red Sea

S

The Sin of Fear

When we review the story in Exodus and Moses' negotiations with Pharaoh, it is interesting to note that Moses insists that the nation of Israel only wants a three day furlough from their labor to worship their God.

> "The elders of Israel will listen to you. Then you and the elders are to go to the king of Egypt and say to him, 'The Lord, the God of the Hebrews, has met with us. Let us take a three-day journey into the desert to offer

sacrifices to the LORD our God.' But I know that the king of Egypt will not let you go unless a mighty hand compels him. So I will stretch out my hand and strike the Egyptians with all the wonders that I will perform among them. After that, he will let you go.

—EXODUS 3:18–20

We have to be reminded over and over that God never intended the Israelites to wander around for forty years in the Sinai wilderness. Remember, it took only two years for them to reach the boundaries of the Promised Land. God was ready for them to take the land! So they sent in the spies.

Amazingly enough, the sin of worshiping the golden calf at the base of Mount Sinai earlier in their journey was not the shortcoming that caused the people to become nomads for a generation. In my book, melting down all of your jewelry to create an idol and worshiping it while your leader is up on a mountain talking with the true God is kind of a big deal. (See Exodus 32:1–3.) And yet, God's plan was still to lead them into the Promised Land. So what was worse than idol worship?

I have often been confused into believing that idolatry was the reason for the elusiveness of the Promised Land for the Israelites. But it was not. It was the Israelites' fear that turned them back.

The sin that built the barrier between those former slaves and their promise was their inaccurate perception of themselves and their God:

They came back to Moses and Aaron and the whole Israelite community at Kadesh in the Desert of Paran. There they reported to them and to the whole assembly and showed them the fruit of the land. They gave Moses this account: "We went into the land to which you sent us, and it does flow with milk and honey!

Here is its fruit. But the people who live there are powerful, and the cities are fortified and very large. We even saw descendants of Anak there. The Amalekites live in the Negev; the Hittites, Jebusites and Amorites live in the hill country; and the Canaanites live near the sea and along the Jordan." Then Caleb silenced the people before Moses and said, "We should go up and take possession of the land, for we can certainly do it." But the men who had gone up with him said, "We can't attack those people; they are stronger than we are." And they spread among the Israelites a bad report about the land they had explored. They said, "The land we explored devours those living in it. All the people we saw there are of great size....*We seemed like grasshoppers in our own eyes, and we looked the same to them.*"

—Numbers 13:26–33, author's emphasis

Death of a Dream

It is a tragic moment. The Israelites stand on the cusp of a new era and the promise of their own land, their own country. Their God has provided for their every need: water, food, safety, and leadership. And now He is about to provide them a home of their own, something they have been promised for centuries. It was to *this* generation that God planned to fulfill his promise. The same feet that walked across the Red Sea floor, the same hands that carried away the gold of the Egyptians, the same eyes that witnessed miracle after miracle, were the same feet, hands, and eyes that would participate in the promise fulfilled. But fear turned them away:

That night all the people of the community raised their voices and wept aloud. All the Israelites grumbled against Moses and Aaron, and the whole assembly

said to them, *"If only we had died in Egypt! Or in this desert! Why is the* LORD *bringing us to this land only to let us fall by the sword?* Our wives and children will be taken as plunder. Wouldn't it be better for us to go back to Egypt?" And they said to each other, "We should choose a leader and go back to Egypt."
—NUMBERS 14:1–4, AUTHOR'S EMPHASIS

From the moment they left Egypt, the Israelites had feared that they would eventually die in the wilderness. Every complaint leveled at Moses was followed by the restatement of that same fear. Now, holding in their hands the grapes of their new home, they cry out their preference for dying in the desert, rather than moving toward God's purpose for them.

Unlike the incident at Mount Sinai with the worship of the golden calf, this sin was too much. They saw themselves as too small to accomplish the work before them and they saw their God as too weak to defend them. God gave the Israelites what they feared, and now what they claimed to prefer. The generation that fled Egypt and basked in God's daily presence and provision would, indeed, die in the desert. Their complaining became a fulfilled prophecy of their own faithless fate. But God, ever merciful, would protect their children from the fear of plunder and raise up a new generation of faithful warriors who would take the land:

So tell them, 'As surely as I live, declares the LORD, *I will do to you the very things I heard you say:* In this desert your bodies will fall—every one of you twenty years old or more who was counted in the census and who has grumbled against me. Not one of you will enter the land I swore with uplifted hand to make your home, except Caleb son of Jephunneh and Joshua son of Nun. As for your children that you said would be

> taken as plunder, I will bring them in to enjoy the land
> you have rejected. But you—your bodies will fall in
> this desert. Your children will be shepherds here for
> forty years, suffering for your unfaithfulness, until the
> last of your bodies lies in the desert.
> —NUMBERS 14:28–33, AUTHOR'S EMPHASIS

God has pronounced that the dream is dead for those that rebelled against Him. What's their response? In typical fashion, the Israelites rebel again. Suddenly, all their fear is gone and they determine to take the land on their own. The dream cannot be dead. One day they perceived themselves as powerless as grasshoppers. The following day, in a desperate attempt to keep their dream alive, they believed themselves to be giants. God warned them that they would fail without His help, but just as fear deafens ears to the voice of God, so does pride:

> Early the next morning they went up toward the high
> hill country. "We have sinned," they said. "We will go
> up to the place the LORD promised." But Moses said,
> "Why are you disobeying the LORD's command? This
> will not succeed! Do not go up, because the LORD is
> not with you. You will be defeated by your enemies,
> for the Amalekites and Canaanites will face you there.
> Because you have turned away from the LORD, he will
> not be with you and you will fall by the sword." Never-
> theless, in their presumption they went up toward the
> high hill country, though neither Moses nor the ark
> of the LORD's covenant moved from the camp. Then
> the Amalekites and Canaanites who lived in that hill
> country came down and attacked them and beat them
> down all the way to Hormah.
> —NUMBERS 14:40–45

DEATH OF FEAR AND PRIDE

Defeat at the hands of their enemies finally convinced the Israelites that the dream was gone, at least for one generation. The death of their dream came quickly, as they were turned back toward the Sinai desert, back from where they came. But the death of that generation's fear and pride would take much more time. It would take the remainder of the forty years, and the rest of Moses' life.

The path between the promise given and the purpose realized is a predictable one. Slaves cannot inherit a kingdom, grasshoppers cannot fight like conquerors, and the rebellious cannot fulfill God's purpose. This path is repeated over and over again in Scripture and is the process by which we take hold of our own purpose in Christ:

> Therefore, brothers, we have an obligation—but it is not to the sinful nature, to live according to it. For if you live according to the sinful nature, you will die; but if by the Spirit you put to death the misdeeds of the body, you will live, because those who are led by the Spirit of God are sons of God. For you did not receive a spirit that makes you a slave again to fear, but you received the Spirit of sonship. And by him we cry, "Abba, Father." The Spirit himself testifies with our spirit that we are God's children. Now if we are children, then we are heirs—heirs of God and co-heirs with Christ, if indeed we share in his sufferings in order that we may also share in his glory.
> —ROMANS 8:12–17

Change Is Easy! It's Transition That's Hard

A couple of years ago I had the unpleasant experience of being employed by a company undergoing a merger. I say unpleasant, but it was really one of the most ugly and stressful periods of my career. Some wise and seasoned person has said, "There are no such things as mergers, only acquisitions." In the corporate world, there is probably no truer statement.

As painful as it was, it was also an incredible lesson on how difficult it is to transition from one identity to another. The experience made me a little more sympathetic to those ragtag slaves that found their way through the desert for two years, but somehow could not bring themselves to believe they could secure their own land.

If there is a guru on change and transition in the corporate world, it has to be William Bridges.[2] As our company was being merged into another, our employees were given the opportunity to take one of Mr. Bridges' video courses called *Managing Transitions* and I was given the opportunity to facilitate the course several times.

Mr. Bridges actually uses the Wilderness Journey as a metaphor for corporate change. His main premise is that change is always external and usually happens in an instant, but transition is our internal response to that change, and the process of transition can take months or even years.

As an example, another company purchased our corporation on July 3, 2002. The external reality of being a new company was completed when all of the papers were signed. It happened in an instant. But the internal response to that reality was a transition that took much longer and happened at a different pace for each person involved. The harder a person struggled against the inevitable changes occurring on a daily basis, the longer it took for the transition to progress and the more pain and loss the person was likely to experience.

That same reality faced the nation of Israel, long before Mr. Bridges or anyone else began theorizing or naming it. The Israelites' freedom was obtained as soon as they left Egypt, but the transition of their identities was a long and painful process. It became longer and more painful than God had intended due to their inability to accept the inevitable path that was before them.

LIVING BEYOND EXERCISE

1. We discussed the journey of Moses and the Israelites through the Sinai desert and how the request to Pharaoh was to release them for only three days so they could worship God. We also discussed how the journey to the Promised Land only took about two years until fear pulled them away for forty years. We called these forty years the death of fear or pride. The process is predictable. Can you use the chart below to identify other people given a vision or dream that went through the same process?

THE PREDICTABLE PATH FROM PROMISE TO PURPOSE

3 DAY DREAM GIVEN		DEATH OF DREAM		DEATH OF FEAR OR PRIDE		PROMISE REALIZED
Moses: Worship God for three days	Crossed sea	Refused to take land	Lost Promise	Forty years in desert	Crossed Jordan	Entered land

2. The vertical lines on the chart represent transitional events between the stages. Can you identify the transitional events in the story of the Israelites

journey from slavery in Egypt to the Promised Land? Can you identify the transitional events for any other people who have taken this path?

3. In the case of the Israelites, two years was not enough to erase the image they had of themselves. They had lived their lives as slaves and could not conceive of themselves as conquering warriors. Remember, it was not the sin of the golden calf that kept them from the promise, it was the sin of believing themselves too small to take the land. This week, take an honest look at how you perceive yourself.

Are there any old labels that remain that hold you back from God's purpose in you?

Are there any fears that you continue to hold on to that prevent you from moving "beyond the frame"?

As we prepare for the next lesson, write down any labels or fears that pull you back from "crossing the river" into what God desires for you.

What shall we say, then? Shall we go on sinning so that grace may increase? By no means! We died to sin; how can we live in it any longer? Or don't you know that all of us who were baptized into Christ Jesus were baptized into his death? We were therefore buried with him through baptism into death in order that, just as Christ was raised from the dead through the glory of the Father, we too may live a new life. If we have been united with him like this in his death, we will certainly also be united with him in his resurrection. For we know that our old self was crucified with him so that the body of sin might be done away with, that we should no longer be slaves to sin—because anyone who has died has been freed from sin.

—ROMANS 6:1–7

CHAPTER 7

From Fearful to Faithful

I<small>N ALL THE</small> studies that I have read on the wilderness journey, the approach is almost invariably from the perspective of God's intervention in the lives of the Israelite nation. Remember the map of the Journey from the previous chapter (page 48)?

The perspective from Moses' life is just as impacting as that of the Israelite nation. The final forty years of Moses' life is spent leading the Israelites through the desert toward the Promised Land and is a reflection of his own spiritual maturity.

You see, he has been there before. The Sinai desert has been his home for forty years, and he has learned the contentment of living there as a free man, when he deserved punishment in Egypt. He has lived the opposite life of the everyday Israelite. Moses was raised with wealth and education. The Israelites were impoverished. Moses committed a crime that was deserving of imprisonment or death in Egypt. The Israelites committed no crime. Moses lived free. The Israelites were enslaved. Moses' life was free from excessive burden. The Israelites were burdened with hard labor and torture for generations. No wonder they didn't appreciate his leadership.

So here is Moses, back again in the Sinai wilderness, worshiping God on the very mountain on which he first approached the burning bush. Do you ever feel like you have been over the same ground before? Moses must have felt that way on at least two specific occasions.

The Legacy of a Prince Turned Criminal

He fled Egypt and Pharaoh to get away from the punishment of defending an Israelite slave. God speaks to him out of the fire and tells him to go back to Egypt to free all of the slaves. Moses must have been wondering, among other things, if this mysterious voice knew of his terrible deeds back home. Didn't he know that he was a murderer and was still on the run? Is it any wonder that Moses tried to talk God out of it? After all, Pharaoh may have a long memory and Moses may still be viewed as a fugitive by both him and his family. Surely when this God from the bush realizes His mistake in picking Moses, He'll find someone else. But Moses doesn't even get the chance to explain to the bush, for the Lord makes a pre-emptive strike:

> Now the LORD had said to Moses in Midian, "Go back to Egypt, for all the men who wanted to kill you are dead."
>
> —EXODUS 4:19

God already knew exactly what Moses had done, and apparently it did not matter. Moses was not disqualified by his past. Only his present response to God's calling could disqualify him, and Moses made a valiant attempt to do just that.

The Legacy of a Shepherd and the Four Lame Excuses

So there he is, standing barefoot in front of the bush and trying to get out of this ridiculous request. Moses provides a whole series of facts that should have provided God with enough evidence that he was the wrong guy for the job. Read the objections as they unfold in the following passages:

#1.

But Moses said to God, "Who am I, that I should go to Pharaoh and bring the Israelites out of Egypt?" And God said, "I will be with you. And this will be the sign to you that it is I who have sent you: When you have brought the people out of Egypt, you will worship God on this mountain." Moses said to God, "Suppose I go to the Israelites and say to them, 'The God of your fathers has sent me to you,' and they ask me, 'What is his name?' Then what shall I tell them?" God said to Moses, "I AM WHO I AM. This is what you are to say to the Israelites: 'I AM has sent me to you.'"

—Exodus 3:11–14

Lack of Identity!

I'm a Nobody

Who ARE you?

Moses answered, "What if they do not believe me or listen to me and say, 'The LORD did not appear to you'?" Then the LORD said to him, "What is that in your hand?" "A staff," he replied. The LORD said, "Throw it on the ground." Moses threw it on the ground and it became a snake, and he ran from it. Then the LORD said to him, "Reach out your hand and take it by the tail." So Moses reached out and took hold of the snake and it turned back into a staff in his hand. "This," said the LORD, "is so that they may believe that the LORD, the God of their fathers—the God of Abraham, the God of Isaac and the God of Jacob—has appeared to you.".... Moses said to the LORD, "O Lord, I have never been eloquent, neither in the past nor since you have spoken to your servant. I am slow of speech and tongue." The LORD said to him, "Who gave man his mouth? Who makes him deaf or mute? Who gives him sight or makes him blind? Is it not I, the LORD? Now go; I will help you speak and will teach you what to say." But Moses said, "O Lord, please send someone else to do it." Then the LORD's anger burned against Moses and he said, "What about your brother, Aaron the Levite? I know he can speak well. He is already on

No credibility

No Skills

his way to meet you, and his heart will be glad when
he sees you.

—EXODUS 4:1–5, 10–14

Moses' objections when he first hears the call of God go
something like this:

"I'm a nobody."

Well, he was once the grandson of Pharaoh, but after forty
years in the desert, he has forgotten all of that. He displays
an amazing lack of self-esteem for someone about to free the
Israelites.

"I do not even know who You are."

Remember, he was raised an Egyptian and has spent the
last forty years taking counsel from his father-in-law who is a
Midian priest, and not an Israelite. The bush is on fire but not
burning up. That's all Moses knows.

**"I have no credibility and the Israelites will not listen to
me."**

No doubt, Moses feared that the Israelites' memories were
as good as Pharaoh's. He cannot believe it himself, and he's
standing in front of the talking bush.

"I lack the necessary skills to lead."

Sheep do not require a conversationalist or a great orator
to lead them. Moses thinks that the Israelites will be more
demanding. If he only knew how demanding, he might have
offered up a stronger excuse.

At every objection God provided Moses with what he
needed. To his self-esteem issues, God simply says, *I'll be
with you.* It is not our worthiness, but God's presence that
enables us to do His will. To Moses' lack of knowledge or
experience with the voice speaking to him out of the bush,
God tells him His name. It does not seem like enough, but

apparently it was enough for Moses to abandon this excuse and move on to the next one. To Moses' lack of credentials, God transforms the tool of Moses' shepherding trade, his staff, into a tool for proving God's validation of Moses' ministry, both to Pharaoh and more importantly, to the Israelite slaves. And finally, in response to Moses' admitted lack of oratory skill, God promises that He will help Moses speak.

In the end, Moses seems to just throw up his hands in frustration and beg for God to send someone, anyone else. God had refuted Moses' four lame excuses of what he lacked: identity, knowledge, authority, and skill. Moses was desperate for a way out. Moses clearly did not believe himself up to the task; it was simply a ludicrous notion. The faltering shepherd and future leader of the Israelites needed someone to help him, so God gave him Aaron.

THE BUILDING OF A LEADER

It is interesting to note that at the beginning of Moses and Aaron's talks with Pharaoh to release the Israelites, Aaron does all the talking. Moses wasn't kidding when he pleaded with God to send someone else. He felt that he was not fully equipped to accomplish all that God had set out for him to do. But he obeyed anyway as he pushed Aaron to the front of the Pharaoh talks. And the obedience, over time and with the issuing of the plagues on the Egyptians, began to build up those missing characteristics, skills, and confidence in Moses. Let's take a closer look at the transformation.

> But Moses said to the LORD, "If the Israelites will not listen to me, why would Pharaoh listen to me, since I speak with faltering lips?"....Now when the LORD spoke to Moses in Egypt, he said to him, "I am the LORD. Tell Pharaoh king of Egypt everything I tell

you." But Moses said to the LORD, "Since I speak with faltering lips, why would Pharaoh listen to me?"

—EXODUS 6:12, 28–30

Then the LORD said to Moses, "See, I have made you like God to Pharaoh, and your brother Aaron will be your prophet. You are to say everything I command you, and your brother Aaron is to tell Pharaoh to let the Israelites go out of his country."

—EXODUS 7:1–2

AARON'S STAFF BECOMES A SNAKE

The LORD said to Moses and Aaron, "When Pharaoh says to you, 'Perform a miracle,' then say to Aaron, 'Take your staff and throw it down before Pharaoh,' and it will become a snake." So Moses and Aaron went to Pharaoh and did just as the LORD commanded. Aaron threw his staff down in front of Pharaoh and his officials, and it became a snake.

—EXODUS 7:8–10

PLAGUE OF BLOOD

The LORD said to Moses, "Tell Aaron, 'Take your staff and stretch out your hand over the waters of Egypt— over the streams and canals, over the ponds and all the reservoirs'—and they will turn to blood. Blood will be everywhere in Egypt, even in the wooden buckets and stone jars." Moses and Aaron did just as the LORD had commanded. He raised his staff in the presence of Pharaoh and his officials and struck the water of the Nile, and all the water was changed into blood.

—EXODUS 7:19–20

PLAGUE OF FROGS

Then the LORD said to Moses, "Tell Aaron, 'Stretch out your hand with your staff over the streams and canals and ponds, and make frogs come up on the land of Egypt.'" So Aaron stretched out his hand over the waters of Egypt, and the frogs came up and covered the land.

—EXODUS 8:5–6

PLAGUE OF GNATS

Then the LORD said to Moses, "Tell Aaron, 'Stretch out your staff and strike the dust of the ground,' and throughout the land of Egypt the dust will become gnats." They did this, and when Aaron stretched out his hand with the staff and struck the dust of the ground, gnats came upon men and animals.

—EXODUS 8:16–17

Now notice what begins to happen during the next plague.

PLAGUE OF FLIES

Then the LORD said to Moses, "Get up early in the morning and confront Pharaoh as he goes to the water and say to him, 'This is what the LORD says: Let my people go, so that they may worship me. If you do not let my people go, I will send swarms of flies on you and your officials, on your people and into your houses....Then Pharaoh summoned Moses and Aaron and said, "Go, sacrifice to your God here in the land." But Moses said, "That would not be right. The sacrifices we offer the LORD our God would be detestable to the Egyptians. And if we offer sacrifices that are detestable in their eyes, will they not stone us? We must take a

three-day journey into the desert to offer sacrifices to
the LORD our God, as he commands us."...Only be
sure that Pharaoh does not act deceitfully again by not
letting the people go to offer sacrifices to the LORD."

—Exodus 8:20–29

Moses has finally found his voice and turns back the sug-
gestion of Pharaoh to make sacrifices inside of Egypt's borders. Moses actually admonishes Pharaoh about his deceitful
behavior.

THE PLAGUE ON LIVESTOCK

Then the LORD said to Moses, "Go to Pharaoh and
say to him, 'This is what the LORD, the God of the
Hebrews, says: "Let my people go, so that they may
worship me." If you refuse to let them go and continue
to hold them back, the hand of the LORD will bring a
terrible plague on your livestock in the field—on your
horses and donkeys and camels and on your cattle and
sheep and goats.

—Exodus 9:1–3

THE PLAGUE OF BOILS

Then the LORD said to Moses and Aaron, "Take hand-
fuls of soot from a furnace and have Moses toss it
into the air in the presence of Pharaoh. It will become
fine dust over the whole land of Egypt, and festering
boils will break out on men and animals throughout
the land." So they took soot from a furnace and stood
before Pharaoh. Moses tossed it into the air, and festering boils broke out on men and animals. The magi-
cians could not stand before Moses because of the
boils that were on them and on all the Egyptians.

—Exodus 9:8–11

THE PLAGUE OF HAIL

Then the LORD said to Moses, "Stretch out your hand toward the sky so that hail will fall all over Egypt— on men and animals and on everything growing in the fields of Egypt." When Moses stretched out his staff toward the sky, the LORD sent thunder and hail, and lightning flashed down to the ground. So the LORD rained hail on the land of Egypt; hail fell and lightning flashed back and forth. It was the worst storm in all the land of Egypt since it had become a nation.

—EXODUS 9:22–24

THE PLAGUE OF LOCUSTS

So Moses stretched out his staff over Egypt, and the LORD made an east wind blow across the land all that day and all that night. By morning the wind had brought the locusts; they invaded all Egypt and settled down in every area of the country in great numbers. Never before had there been such a plague of locusts, nor will there ever be again.

—EXODUS 10:13–14

On this particular occasion, Pharaoh attempts to negotiate with Moses by allowing him to take only the men to worship God. Moses stands firm and refuses Pharaoh the compromise on this plague and the following.

THE PLAGUE OF DARKNESS

Then the LORD said to Moses, "Stretch out your hand toward the sky so that darkness will spread over Egypt—darkness that can be felt." So Moses stretched out his hand toward the sky, and total

67

darkness covered all Egypt for three days.
—EXODUS 10:21–22

This time Pharaoh was willing to let women and children worship with the men of Israel, but now Moses is a leader with confidence that God's way is the only way. Again, it is Moses who is now receiving the instruction from God and delivering the message himself.

THE PLAGUE ON THE FIRSTBORN

So Moses said, "This is what the LORD says: 'About midnight I will go throughout Egypt. Every firstborn son in Egypt will die, from the firstborn son of Pharaoh, who sits on the throne, to the firstborn son of the slave girl, who is at her hand mill, and all the firstborn of the cattle as well....All these officials of yours will come to me, bowing down before me and saying, 'Go, you and all the people who follow you!' After that I will leave." Then Moses, hot with anger, left Pharaoh.
—EXODUS 11:4–5, 8

Now this is a transformed Moses. You can almost hear the change in voice tone when you read the passages together. Moses seems to deliver the message with gusto!

It is unclear whether or not Moses miraculously lost his speech impediment, but it does not seem to matter either way. The condition of Moses' heart and belief has been altered. One wonders if the plagues were intended to convince Pharaoh or if they were meant for Moses. By the time the tenth plague was pronounced, the Israelites had enough confidence in Moses to follow his instructions and follow his footsteps out of Egypt. Without his personal transformation, it seems unlikely that the slaves would have ever left to follow a man that perceived himself as only a shepherd or fugitive. No, a change in vocation required a change in identity.

A New Man, a New Responsibility

Mission accomplished, right? Moses did it! The Israelites are free from the Egyptians and within a couple of months they are all standing at the foot of the same mountain on which Moses first met up with the burning bush. He is a transformed Moses who is revisiting that sacred place to speak with God again and receive His words for the people. Truly, it had to have been a "mountaintop experience" like no other. And Moses' badges of courage and obedience would be those stone tablets he would carry down with him. The Israelites were free!

One might think it was time for a little vacation for the new leader. But he hears something down the mountain and he must attend to it.

There are thousands of Israelites down below, encircling and worshiping a calf made of the same gold that recently encircled their wrists and ankles. Moses responds differently then the Moses who pleaded with God to let someone else lead the Israelites. Moses is now fully capable of handling the situations that arise with the authority and power of the God who called him. There is even a hint of the young Moses who stood in the face of danger and defended the Israelite slave from the Egyptian oppressor. Can you see a bit of the younger Moses as you read in Exodus 32:

> Then the LORD said to Moses, "Go down, because your people, whom you brought up out of Egypt, have become corrupt. They have been quick to turn away from what I commanded them and have made themselves an idol cast in the shape of a calf....Now leave me alone so that my anger may burn against them and

that I may destroy them. Then I will make you into a great nation." But Moses sought the favor of the LORD his God. "O LORD," he said, "why should your anger burn against your people, whom you brought out of Egypt with great power and a mighty hand?...Turn from your fierce anger; relent and do not bring disaster on your people....Then the LORD relented and did not bring on his people the disaster he had threatened.

—EXODUS 32:7–8, 10–11, 12, 14

The passion to defend and protect his people has returned to Moses, but this time it is with God's calling and not his own will. God's presence has transformed him. One of the most ironic phrases in this passage is in verse 7, where God refers to the Israelites as "your people" to Moses and proclaims that Moses was the one who brought them out of Egypt. Although the mountain is the same, Moses now knows intimately the God speaking to him. Moses now shares His identity, His name, His power, His authority and most of all, His presence. The four lame excuses have disappeared and in their place a certain confidence has grown; a confidence that only time with God could have inspired, and only obedience to Him could have nurtured. Moses has been faithful to both.

LIVING BEYOND EXERCISE

1. Using the four lame excuses as categories, what excuses have you been using to disqualify yourself from fulfilling God's purpose?

LACK OF IDENTITY	LACK OF GODLY KNOWLEDGE	LACK OF AUTHORITY	LACK OF SKILL

2. When Moses pleaded with God to find someone else, God provided him with someone to help in the form of his brother, Aaron. Has God brought you any "partners" or those that would strengthen you in areas where you might feel you are weak? List those people and describe how they contribute to your life, ministry, and confidence. Remember to include people from your past as well as the present.

3. One of the excuses Moses gave to God was that he lacked the authority to lead the Israelites. God's response was to ask Moses, "What is that in your hand?" (Exod. 4:2). In Moses' case, he was holding a staff, a common tool used by shepherds. God used that common tool for His uncommon purposes throughout Moses' ministry. If God were to ask you "What is that in your hand?" what would your answer be? Make a list, or take a personal inventory, of everything that you have that could potentially be used by God. The inventory can include gifts, abilities, relationships, personal assets, or past experiences.

PERSONAL INVENTORY
(WHAT IS IN YOUR HAND?)

Gifts

good | Bad.
Things you don't want others to see.

Abilities

Relationships

Assets

Experiences

CHAPTER 8

Regret and Remembrance

A GENERATION HAS PASSED away, their whole lives eating manna instead of grapes; forty years instead of the intended two years living on the sand. The very fear that consumed the Israelites was the very thing that eventually came to pass. Do you remember their cries and complaints to Moses and each other? Their fear of others and their lack of fear of God condemned them to wander around knowing they would never eat anything but manna and have their final resting place in the sand. Unfulfilled promise—can there be a worse fate? Imagine it for yourself for a moment. Every meal, every step, every moment, knowing you were destined to be somewhere else and missing it by such a short distance.

If you have seen the movie *Apollo 13* you can get a small glimpse of the magnitude of that kind of disappointment. The movie is based on the historical events depicted in the book *Lost Moon* by Jim Lovell, the captain of that mission. Although the astronauts were brought back safely, the purpose for all those years of training and preparation to land on the moon was not achieved. It was to be Jim Lovell's last space flight, and according to him, his most memorable and heartbreaking. You see, when you know your destination and prepare for it so thoroughly, *not* making it can make such a strong impact that it becomes more memorable than any accomplishments that occurred before or after.

THE RACE NOT RUN

I was a sprinter in high school. To look at me and my short legs, you would never know it. But a sprinter I was, and definitely not a long distance runner. If the distance was much longer than one hundred meters, my desire and endurance waned quickly. As luck and genetics would have it, I was a pretty good sprinter and my favorite race was the four hundred meter relay.

The four hundred meter or "short" relay is an interesting race. It involves four runners exchanging a baton to complete one lap around the track. It is a team race in what is usually an individual sport. I loved this race! Each hundred-meter leg is really more like 120 meters because during the baton exchange, two runners run together. For a brief moment those two runners share both the responsibility of the race and the baton. It is the best and most difficult part of the race. It is where relay races are won and lost.

The trick, if you are the runner receiving the baton, is to start running as fast as you can without leaving too early to outrun your teammate and therefore, miss the baton, and at the same time, not leaving too late to have that same teammate overtake you and run up your backside with spiked shoes. All of this must be accomplished within the confines of two stripes across the lane measuring only twenty meters apart. The exchange must occur between those two lines, or the runners are disqualified.

If you miss the baton because you took off too soon, the entire team is disqualified because a runner cannot advance to the next exchange without the baton. But if you delay the take off too long to avoid the catastrophe of missing the baton and being disqualified, your team is not likely to win the race. The delay will cost you valuable fractions of a second and the spike holes on your heels and calves won't help your time, either. The wounds of disqualification, the wounds of a slow time, and spikes—the goal is to win the race by avoiding all of them.

I lettered all four years of high school and picked up quite a few medals and ribbons along the way. And how fast was our team? We were even state champions one year with a record-breaking time. I also ran the one hundred meters, the two hundred meters (way too long; I did not like that race at all), and dabbled in long jump. I do not know how many races I ran during those years, but it had to be hundreds. Every race, frankly, is a blur. Of all the races I ran, I do not remember any one of those races specifically—except for one in particular.

It was the last race I would run. It was my senior year at the state track meet. We were slated to at least medal, but had a good chance of placing in the top two teams. We needed to run fast and more importantly, pass well without errors. We practiced those exchanges for hours, mornings and evenings, before the final meet of the year. Practice, practice, practice.

I anchored that year, meaning I would be the last runner to receive the baton and I would be the one to carry it across the finish line and lunge forward toward the red tape stretched across the lanes at the end. I would have to wait patiently through three other runners on my team and their two baton exchanges before my exchange and subsequent leg of the race would begin. It is excruciating to wait.

Unfortunately, I did not have to wait very long to see what the outcome of our team's efforts would be. The first runner took off and ran her leg of the race well. But as I said before, the race is won or lost in the exchanges. So it was with our team. As I stood there and watched the two runners struggle and finally lose the first pass, I was heartbroken. We were disqualified. Because other teams needed to finish their race, the disqualified runners on our team were required to stay in our lane until the race was over and a winner declared. It was horrible. I waited for the third leg runner of our team to reach me, not at the planned sprint, but rather at a slow and dejected walk, then we walked together in our lane, consoling each other, to the finish line.

It is a horrible memory, but one which I remember down to the most minute detail. Just writing it down brings about the same gut-wrenching disappointment of that afternoon. All of that practice on the exchanges ended with that one failed exchange. I have often asked God why it was the one race that I remember so well in the crowd of other races long forgotten; the race I did not even run.

In life, everyone runs. Not the same race always, but one marked out just for us. Sometimes we can get caught up in trying to figure out how to run the race perfectly. I can begin to rely on my own speed, my own giftedness, my own technique. If I am not paying attention, I sometimes get so distracted with improving myself and my "time" that I stop running the race altogether. It is hardly noticeable. I mean, practice looks a lot like the real thing, doesn't it? But practicing the race is not running the race. It is merely rehearsing it. God calls us to *run*—not to rehearse.

> Therefore, since we are surrounded by such a great cloud of witnesses, let us throw off everything that hinders and the sin that so easily entangles, and let us run with perseverance the race marked out for us. Let us fix our eyes on Jesus, the author and perfecter of our faith, who for the joy set before him endured the cross, scorning its shame, and sat down at the right hand of the throne of God.
> —Hebrews 12:1–2

So there are the Israelites. Thanks to their parents' lack of belief and trust, they have been "practicing" in the Sinai Desert for forty years while their dream continued to be deferred, the race God had chosen for them yet to be run. They have had a few little skirmishes out there and have practiced a little art of war, but the real thing, the real dream was still ahead.

When the last of the doubters and Egyptian slaves pass away and only warriors remain, it is time to make the journey that has been postponed. Can you imagine the anticipation? Had some of the Israelites grown accustomed to practicing like their parents had grown accustomed to slavery? It does not appear so... the memory of the race not run is too strong.

And then there is Moses. He was 120 years old and preparing to hand over the mantle of leadership and the realization of the dream into another's hand. Can you see the baton in Moses' hand? Moses and Jacob have run this race together for a period of time but now Moses must let go and the Israelites must prepare to leave this familiar place without him.

THE LAST WORD

The people all wait to hear Moses' parting words. They know that they will be very important words, as most parting words tend to be. His last words of encouragement and fatherly advice will be the words still ringing in their ears and hearts as they battle for the land they have dreamed of for their entire lives. The rehearsing is soon to be over. There has never been a more "captive" audience than those awaiting Moses' pre-battle instructions. Moses himself must realize that these words and this message will be his last and most lasting. So what does he talk about?

Interestingly enough, Moses does not talk about battle strategies or remind them of how to wield a sword. His words are not filled with encouragement to fight hard or follow their commanders faithfully. There is no mention of the wives and children needing to support the troops during the war effort.

Instead, Moses gives them a history lesson that lasts the entire Book of Deuteronomy; God's provision and caring in exchange for the Israelites' forgetfulness and faithlessness. With every word and phrase he reminds them of how God has touched them, cared for them, intervened for them, loved them, fed them, corrected them, and endured them.

With their eyes looking toward their future, their fulfilled promise, their ears and hearts burn with the memories of a God who loves them. It is the memory of those places where God has performed miracles in their lives that will keep their own hearts faithful and obedient for their next journey into battles for the land. No battle drills today, only memory drills. God and Moses both know that people are forgetful. Look how easy it was for those whose feet passed through the Red Sea to forget that their God was with them? How long did it take, two days? How much more might these children of that generation forget what God did?

And here is the lesson. A good memory of God's power, presence, and love in the past is the most important armament for our future calling and fulfillment of His promise!

It humbles us: We will remember that God has accomplished it all!

It empowers us: We will remember that if God calls us to it, He will accomplish it again.

It removes fear: We will remember that God's presence and power is in us and we will be far less likely to make "grasshoppers" out of God's chosen.

It humbles us again: We will remember that future victories and glories belong to Him alone.

THE MEMORY IS THE FIRST TO GO

It's an old joke, one that everyone can appreciate at one time or another. How many times have you walked into a room and forgotten why you were there? Or, as some of my closest friends like to point out: how many times in a month do I forget where I have placed my keys or cell phone? Admit it. You have had to dial your own cell phone number from another phone just hoping there was enough battery power left to make it ring so you could locate it! There is a phrase that my husband likes to use: "My memory is very, very good…it's just very, very short!" It is in our nature to forget, and God knows it.

When God wants us to remember an encounter, he sometimes leaves us a little sticky note to remind us of His presence and provision. In the Old Testament, the reminder note was usually left in the form of a large rock or pile of stones. Of course, rocks were pretty common in that region (about as common as sticky notes today), so it is no wonder. Here are a few examples of stones or rocks left as reminders of a person's encounter with God or an understanding between people.

JACOB RECEIVES A PROMISE

Jacob left Beersheba and set out for Haran. When he reached a certain place, he stopped for the night because the sun had set. Taking one of the stones there, he put it under his head and lay down to sleep. He had a dream in which he saw a stairway resting on the earth, with its top reaching to heaven, and the angels of God were ascending and descending on it. There above it stood the LORD, and he said: "I am the LORD, the God of your father Abraham and the God of Isaac….When Jacob awoke from his sleep, he thought, "Surely the LORD is in this place, and I was not aware of it."...Early the next morning Jacob took the stone he had placed under his head and set it up as a pillar and poured oil on top of it....Then Jacob made a vow, saying, "If God will be with me and will watch over me on this journey I am taking and will give me food to eat and clothes to wear so that I return safely to my father's house, then the LORD will be my God and this stone that I have set up as a pillar will be God's house, and of all that you give me I will give you a tenth."

—GENESIS 28:10–13, 16, 18, 20–22

JACOB RECEIVES A NEW NAME

After Jacob returned from Paddan Aram, God appeared to him again and blessed him. God said to him, "Your name is Jacob, but you will no longer be called Jacob; your name will be Israel." So he named him Israel. And God said to him, "I am God Almighty...A nation and a community of nations will come from you, and kings will come from your body. The land I gave to Abraham and Isaac I also give to you, and I will give this land to your descendants after you." Then God went up from him at the place where he had talked with him. Jacob set up a stone pillar at the place where God had talked with him, and he poured out a drink offering on it; he also poured oil on it.

—GENESIS 35:9–14

GOD'S COVENANT WRITTEN ON STONES

Then the LORD spoke to you out of the fire. You heard the sound of words but saw no form; there was only a voice. He declared to you his covenant, the Ten Commandments, which he commanded you to follow and then wrote them on two stone tablets. And the LORD directed me at that time to teach you the decrees and laws you are to follow in the land that you are crossing the Jordan to possess.

—DEUTERONOMY 4:12–14

COVENANT BETWEEN NEIGHBORS

Do not move your neighbor's boundary stone set up by your predecessors in the inheritance you receive in the land the LORD your God is giving you to possess.

—DEUTERONOMY 19:14

REMINDER OF THE JORDAN CROSSING

So Joshua called together the twelve men he had appointed from the Israelites, one from each tribe, and said to them, "Go over before the ark of the LORD your God into the middle of the Jordan. Each of you is to take up a stone on his shoulder, according to the number of the tribes of the Israelites, to serve as a sign among you. In the future, when your children ask you, 'What do these stones mean?' tell them that the flow of the Jordan was cut off before the ark of the covenant of the LORD. When it crossed the Jordan, the waters of the Jordan were cut off. These stones are to be a memorial to the people of Israel forever."

—JOSHUA 4:4–7

ISRAEL RENEWS THEIR COVENANT WITH GOD

And the people said to Joshua, "We will serve the LORD our God and obey him." On that day Joshua made a covenant for the people, and there at Shechem he drew up for them decrees and laws. And Joshua recorded these things in the Book of the Law of God. Then he took a large stone and set it up there under the oak near the holy place of the LORD. "See!" he said to all the people. "This stone will be a witness against us. It has heard all the words the LORD has said to us. It will be a witness against you if you are untrue to your God."

—JOSHUA 24:24–27

A REMINDER OF GOD'S PROTECTION

Then Samuel took a stone and set it up between Mizpah and Shen. He named it Ebenezer, saying, "Thus far has the LORD helped us." So the Philistines were subdued and did not invade Israelite territory again.

—1 SAMUEL 7:12–13

Stones and rocks are so ordinary, yet there is also something very God-like in that common form of remembrance. Something so readily available and commonplace becomes a spiritual landmark in the hands of God. Isn't that the story of our lives? We can have events happen to us that may be commonplace, not miraculous at all. But in the hands of God, they can become reminders that God has been with us and has made a miraculous difference.

So Moses recounts the stones and stories where God has touched them. He makes them remember. Before they cross the river toward their future, Moses helps them remember everything God has done in their past and to whom their future belongs.

The memory lesson is so important that after the history lesson, God admits that the people will forget as soon as the battles are over and the land has been won. They will still forget! So for added measure, God instructs Moses to sing them a song so they will remember even after they have forgotten their God again:

"Now write down for yourselves this song and teach it to the Israelites and have them sing it, so that it may be a witness for me against them. When I have brought them into the land flowing with milk and honey, the land I promised on oath to their forefathers, and when they eat their fill and thrive, they will turn to other gods and worship them, rejecting me and breaking my covenant. And when many disasters and difficulties come upon them, this song will testify against them, because it will not be forgotten by their descendants. I know what they are disposed to do, even before I bring them into the land I promised them on oath." So Moses wrote down this song that day and taught it to the Israelites.

—Deuteronomy 31:19–22

When Moses finished reciting all these words to all Israel, he said to them, "Take to heart all the words I have solemnly declared to you this day, so that you may command your children to obey carefully all the words of this law. They are not just idle words for you—they are your life. By them you will live long in the land you are crossing the Jordan to possess."

—Deuteronomy 32:45–47

The words of remembering are life! Whether our memories come to us through song or through stone, the memories of God's provision in our lives are not idle, they are life. Before we grasp the taking and the keeping of God's promise, we must remember what He has done. Every stone of the Israelite history is turned. The song has been sung. And with that, the baton is passed and the race for Moses ends.

LIVING BEYOND EXERCISE

1. Review how many times Moses calls the Israelites to "remember" or admonishes them to "not forget" before crossing the river:

Only be careful, and watch yourselves closely so that you *do not forget* the things your eyes have seen or let them slip from your heart as long as you live. Teach them to your children and to their children after them.
—DEUTERONOMY 4:9

Remember the day you stood before the LORD your God at Horeb.
—DEUTERONOMY 4:10

Be careful *not* to *forget* the covenant of the LORD your God that he made with you; do not make for yourselves an idol in the form of anything the LORD your God has forbidden.
—DEUTERONOMY 4:23

Remember that you were slaves in Egypt and that the LORD your God brought you out of there with a mighty hand and an outstretched arm.
—DEUTERONOMY 5:15

Be careful that you *do not forget* the LORD, who brought you out of Egypt, out of the land of slavery.
—DEUTERONOMY 6:12

But do not be afraid of them; *remember* well what the LORD your God did to Pharaoh and to all Egypt.
—DEUTERONOMY 7:18

Remember how the LORD your God led you all the way in the desert these forty years, to humble you and to test you in order to know what was in your heart, whether or not you would keep his commands.

—DEUTERONOMY 8:2

Be careful that you *do not forget* the LORD your God, failing to observe his commands, his laws and his decrees that I am giving you this day.

—DEUTERONOMY 8:11

But *remember* the LORD your God, for it is he who gives you the ability to produce wealth, and so confirms his covenant, which he swore to your forefathers, as it is today.

—DEUTERONOMY 8:18

Remember this and never forget how you provoked the LORD your God to anger in the desert.

—DEUTERONOMY 9:7

Remember today that your children were not the ones who saw and experienced the discipline of the LORD your God: his majesty, his mighty hand, his outstretched arm.

—DEUTERONOMY 11:2

Remember that you were slaves in Egypt and the LORD your God redeemed you.

—DEUTERONOMY 15:15

Do not eat it with bread made with yeast, but for seven days eat unleavened bread, the bread of affliction, because you left Egypt in haste—so that all the days of your life you may *remember* the time of your departure from Egypt.

—DEUTERONOMY 16:3

Remember that you were slaves in Egypt, and follow carefully these decrees.

—Deuteronomy 16:12

Remember what the Lord your God did to Miriam along the way after you came out of Egypt.

—Deuteronomy 24:9

Remember that you were slaves in Egypt and the Lord your God redeemed you from there.

—Deuteronomy 24:18

Remember that you were slaves in Egypt. That is why I command you to do this.

—Deuteronomy 24:22

Remember what the Amalekites did to you along the way when you came out of Egypt.

—Deuteronomy 25:17

When the Lord your God gives you rest from all the enemies around you in the land he is giving you to possess as an inheritance, you shall blot out the memory of Amalek from under heaven. *Do not forget!*

—Deuteronomy 25:19

Remember the days of old; consider the generations long past. Ask your father and he will tell you, your elders, and they will explain to you.

—Deuteronomy 32:7

STONES OF REMEMBRANCE

2. The following exercise is best when done over a long period of time. The first time I did this the process lasted several months and I was completely blessed by all that God graciously revealed. Be patient.

Try to recall your history with God. You can use a timeline or actually use physical stones for this exercise. Just start with blank sheets of paper taped end to end with bold lines to represent each year of your life. In some ways, it will be like the Wheel of Life used in Chapter 5, only with the timeline you will have much more room to write.

Where are the obvious "stones of remembrance" that have been left to serve as a reminder of His presence, provision, and power in your life? Mark those places on your timeline. There are probably a few very obvious large stones that are easy to remember. If you are using a timeline, be sure to place large marks on the appropriate year of your life where those events have occurred and label them.

Now pray. Ask God to reveal to you those places or events where you might have forgotten what He has done or maybe never knew that His hand was present.

CHAPTER 9

The Study of Stones

THROUGHOUT THE LAST few chapters, we have been discussing the importance of remembering what God has done. We have also discovered that often, because we have a difficult time remembering, God leaves His mark to help draw us back to His glory. In dealing with the nation of Israel, God used stones, because that was what was around. They were plentiful. They were common.

In our everyday lives, God is leaving stones to help remind us to look toward Him, to remember what He has done, to remember that He has taken the ordinary "stones" of our lives and made them holy by His power and presence. A few examples:

- A common hillside bush catches fire with God's presence and the place becomes holy ground.

- An ordinary shepherd's crook becomes a snake under the extraordinary power of God.

- A child's lunch becomes a feast for thousands through God's blessing.

Wherever the presence of God is, common objects are used for uncommon purposes and ordinary people accomplish extraordinary things for the kingdom of God. Let's take a look at the different uses for stones in our everyday lives and draw out some spiritual lessons from those uses. Try not to "spiritualize" the uses until you have fully exhausted all of the types of stones in your experiences. To assist in the thought process, divide up the types of stones by size like on the grid provided below. One use has been filled in for each size to get you started.

Common Uses of Stones and Uncommon Lessons

SIZE	COMMON USES	SPIRITUAL LESSONS
TINY	Sand	Filtering impurities
SMALL	Used in landscaping	Adds beauty and interest
MEDIUM	Used around firepits	Protects
LARGE	Retention walls	Holds back dirt

The very first time I taught this particular lesson, I divided the group into four and encouraged each group to take one of the sizes and brainstorm on the common uses only. It was actually difficult for them not to draw spiritual analogies right away and want to talk about them in their small group. After all of the groups had exhausted their ideas, all of the groups came together and began discussing the spiritual implications of the common uses of stones. It was an amazing time of insight and heightened awareness of what is meant by the recounting of the triumphal entry as told in Luke:

> When he came near the place where the road goes down the Mount of Olives, the whole crowd of disciples began joyfully to praise God in loud voices for all the miracles they had seen: "Blessed is the king who comes in the name of the Lord!" "Peace in heaven and glory in the highest!" Some of the Pharisees in the crowd said to Jesus, "Teacher, rebuke your disciples!" "I tell you," he replied, "*if they keep quiet, the stones will cry out.*"
>
> —LUKE 19:37–40, AUTHOR'S EMPHASIS

The stones do cry out praise and worship, if we only stop long enough to listen. God has put the message of His glory in everything that He has created, even something as common as a stone or rock. It is not by accident. Over and over again the inspired writers of both the Old and New Testament have used stones to remember Him, and to describe His attributes.

Moses

> He is the Rock, his works are perfect, and all his ways are just. A faithful God who does no wrong, upright and just is he.
>
> —DEUTERONOMY 32:4

Hannah

> There is no one holy [Or no Holy One] like the LORD; there is no one besides you; there is no Rock like our God.
>
> —1 SAMUEL 2:2, AUTHOR'S PARAPHRASE

David

David sang to the LORD the words of this song when the LORD delivered him from the hand of all his enemies and from the hand of Saul. He said: "The LORD is my rock, my fortress and my deliverer; my God is my rock, in whom I take refuge, my shield and the horn of my salvation. He is my stronghold, my refuge and my savior- from violent men you save me. I call to the LORD, who is worthy of praise, and I am saved from my enemies.

—2 SAMUEL 22:1–4

Prophet Isaiah

Trust in the LORD forever, for the LORD, the LORD, is the *Rock* eternal.

—ISAIAH 26:4

Daniel prophesying to King Nebuchadnezzar

"In the time of those kings, the God of heaven will set up a kingdom that will never be destroyed, nor will it be left to another people. It will crush all those kingdoms and bring them to an end, but it will itself endure forever. This is the meaning of the vision of the rock cut out of a mountain, but not by human hands-a rock that broke the iron, the bronze, the clay, the silver and the gold to pieces. "The great God has shown the king what will take place in the future. The dream is true and the interpretation is trustworthy."

—DANIEL 2:44–45

Paul the Apostle

What then shall we say? That the Gentiles, who did not pursue righteousness, have obtained it, a righteousness that is by faith; but Israel, who pursued a law of righteousness, has not attained it. Why not? Because they pursued it not by faith but as if it were by works. They stumbled over the "stumbling stone." As it is written: "See, I lay in Zion a stone that causes men to stumble and a rock that makes them fall, and the one who trusts in him will never be put to shame."

—ROMANS 9:30–33

Paul is paraphrasing Isaiah 18 in this passage, but Isaiah had another, even more descriptive prophecy regarding God as "stone":

So this is what the Sovereign LORD says: "See, I lay a stone in Zion, a tested stone, a precious *cornerstone* for a sure foundation; the one who trusts will never be dismayed."

—ISAIAH 28:16, AUTHOR'S EMPHASIS

CORNERSTONE AND CAPSTONE

Even Jesus describes Himself to the religious leaders by quoting Psalm 118.

Jesus looked directly at them and asked, "Then what is the meaning of that which is written: "'The stone the builders rejected has become the capstone'? Everyone who falls on that stone will be broken to pieces, but he on whom it falls will be crushed." The teachers of the law and the chief priests looked for a way to arrest him immediately, because they knew he had spoken this parable against them. But they were afraid of the people. Keeping a close watch on him, they sent spies, who pretended to be honest. They hoped to catch Jesus in something he said so that they might hand him over to the power and authority of the governor.

—LUKE 20:17–20

The words *capstone* and *cornerstone* are usually used synonymously but neither are words we use every day, so a definition is helpful—capstone: a stone at the corner of a building uniting two intersecting walls.

If Jesus is considered the capstone or cornerstone of a "building" that God has constructed, what are the two walls that are intersecting? The religious leaders knew exactly what Jesus was saying in regards to Himself, which is why they immediately began to make plans to arrest Him. Jesus proclaimed Himself the Cornerstone that connected the two walls of His redemption, the Israelites and the Gentiles, those with His Word and Law, and those without:

> As you come to him, the living Stone-rejected by men but chosen by God and precious to him—you also, like living stones, are being built into a spiritual house to be a holy priesthood, offering spiritual sacrifices acceptable to God through Jesus Christ. For in Scripture it says: "See, I lay a stone in Zion, a chosen and precious cornerstone, and the one who trusts in him will never be put to shame." Now to you who believe, this stone is precious. But to those who do not believe, "The stone the builders rejected has become the capstone," and, "A stone that causes men to stumble and a rock that makes them fall." They stumble because they disobey the message—which is also what they were destined for.
>
> —1 Peter 2:4–8

A Collision Course

It is as if all of history, both Godly and ungodly, those with the law and those without the law, have been on a collision course from the beginning of recorded time. Although far apart in the beginning like two perpendicular walls of a building, Israelites and Gentiles were always headed toward the same intersection, the intersection of the cornerstone of Jesus Christ. From the very first separation of man from God, there was His plan to reconcile *all* people to Himself. It is the collision at the cross!

> And I will put enmity between you and the woman, and between your offspring and hers; he will crush your head, and you will strike his heel.
>
> —GENESIS 3:15

God repeats His commitment to be reconciled to all people when He establishes His covenant with Abraham, after Abraham is faithful in his willingness to be obedient and sacrifice his son Isaac.

> The angel of the LORD called to Abraham from heaven a second time and said, "I swear by myself, declares the LORD, that because you have done this and have not withheld your son, your only son, I will surely bless you and make your descendants as numerous as the stars in the sky and as the sand on the seashore. Your descendants will take possession of the cities of their enemies, and through your offspring all nations on earth will be blessed, because you have obeyed me."
>
> —GENESIS 22:15–18

Just as there was a collision course of all nations at the cornerstone of Jesus, there is also a collision course set for every human heart. Every person has the "Gentile Way" and the "Israelite Way" working inside of them, drawing them toward the saving Gospel of Jesus Christ. There are things that we have done that we would consider "good" or righteous, decisions or actions of which we could be proud. This could be considered the Godly way, the way of God's Law, the

"Israelite Way." There are also actions or decisions that each of us has made that do not reflect God's law or desires for us, but our own desires. Perhaps we would even describe them as "bad" decisions. We might be ashamed of these actions or at least ashamed of the results. They could be considered the "Gentile Way."

Perhaps this is what Paul meant when he said:

> But the gift is not like the trespass. For if the many died by the trespass of the one man, how much more did God's grace and the gift that came by the grace of the one man, Jesus Christ, overflow to the many! Again, the gift of God is not like the result of the one man's sin: The judgment followed one sin and brought condemnation, but the gift followed many trespasses and brought justification. For if, by the trespass of the one man, death reigned through that one man, how much more will those who receive God's abundant provision of grace and of the gift of righteousness reign in life through the one man, Jesus Christ. Consequently, just as the result of one trespass was condemnation for all men, so also *the result of one act of righteousness was justification that brings life for all men.* For just as through the disobedience of the one man the many were made sinners, so also through the obedience of the one man the many will be made righteous.
> —Romans 5:15–19, author's emphasis

Just like the one righteous act of obedience from Abraham in his willingness to sacrifice his son, Isaac, resulted in the blessing to all nations, the righteous act of Jesus Christ brings all things in our own lives into God's justification. There is no longer shame or a need to hide the "bad" or exalt the "good" of our old heritage, environment, behavior, capabilities, beliefs, or identity. We have a new identity in the Cornerstone of Jesus Christ that brings both "Gentile" and "Israelite" cultures of our heart under His righteousness.

SAME ROCK, DIFFERENT RESULTS

Regardless of what lies within our past, if we place our trust in Him we will be saved. Reconciliation of all people is the highest purpose of God as "Rock." How does a rock save?

Many years ago I used to attend a camp located near a river. There was a nice, calm, swimming hole where all the campers were allowed to swim. As my friends and I got older we began to venture down river to where the water ran more swiftly. There was a section of the river, however, that was so swift that it was a challenge to navigate without getting a little banged up on the way down. The river was shallow enough that the rocks below the surface would scrape against your feet and legs as you passed them on the rapid current. There was only one way to successfully make it to the next swimming hole without cuts and bruises. You see, in the middle of the roughest water and sharpest turn, there was a big rock. If you were smart enough to grab it and keep hold, you could actually crawl onto it and climb over to the other side and avoid the shallowest and most dangerous part of the current. If you did not manage to grab it, you were destined to bang up against it with quite a bit of impact, and your legs would be victims to all the other rocks under the water. The big rock was the rock that saved! Our God is a really big Rock—if we hold on to Him, we will be saved.

> The LORD is my *rock*, my fortress and my deliverer; my God is my *rock*, in whom I take refuge. He is my shield and the horn of my salvation [*horn* symbolizes strength], my stronghold.
> —PSALM 18:2, AUTHOR'S EMPHASES

But look what happens to those who have forgotten what God has done, as when Isaiah prophesied over the two kingdoms of Israel:

> The Lord Almighty is the one you are to regard as holy, he is the one you are to fear, he is the one you are to dread, and he will be a sanctuary; but for both houses of Israel he will be a stone that causes men to stumble and a rock that makes them fall. And for the people of Jerusalem he will be a trap and a snare. Many of them will stumble; they will fall and be broken, they will be snared and captured.
>
> —Isaiah 8:13–15

It's the same rock! One time it is used to save, the other to discipline. The very rock that was intended to save us will also cause us to "stumble." Have you ever tripped over a raised crack in the sidewalk? What is your immediate reaction? I don't know about you, but I immediately look down and attempt to discover what has caused me to stumble. It is a natural reaction, even if you already know that it was a bump in the sidewalk.

God's intention is to discipline, rather than destroy. When we are going in the wrong direction, He attempts to get our attention by causing us to stumble, to slow down and take a closer look.

And what do you do once you have discovered the cause of your stumbling? If I have already stumbled once, I am much more conscientious about each step I take afterward. That is the spiritual purpose of the "stumbling stone." If we are not reaching out for Him as our Rock, then He attempts to "trip us up" in order to get us to take notice of where we are and be more careful, so that we will continue on the right path, on His path.

Jesus as Rock is the Cornerstone of all the events, good and bad, that have taken place. Every decision made and every path we have taken so far intersects at the Rock called Jesus. We can choose to reach out to Him and be saved, or continue to get scratched up by the rocks that lie beneath the surface of the swift waters of our lives. The difference between this river and the one from my childhood is that this river comes round that rock over and over again. If you choose to pass it by on this trip, you will see it again. As long as there is life, the Rock is somewhere in the middle of it, offering refuge for those who are willing to reach out and grab it.

LIVING BEYOND EXERCISE

1. Using the pyramid on the next page, visualize the cross acting as the cornerstone to the two intersecting lines of "God's Way" and "World's Way." You can also use the terms "Israelite" and "Gentile" if you prefer. First, write in the six categories previously discussed: heritage, environment, behavior, capabilities, beliefs, and identity. Now, write down those things that you might be tempted to be ashamed of or proud of from your past and place them on the appropriate side of the pyramid. For example, let's say that you smoke cigarettes and are embarrassed by this behavior. You used to not care, but now that you are going to church, you have become self-conscious of it. You would place the word *smoke* on the behavior line on the left side of the dividing line. If you have memorized and can recite the twenty-third Psalm, you might be proud of that accomplishment and place that on the capabilities line on the right side of the line. Take your time and try to think of everything that might impact how you see yourself and your past.

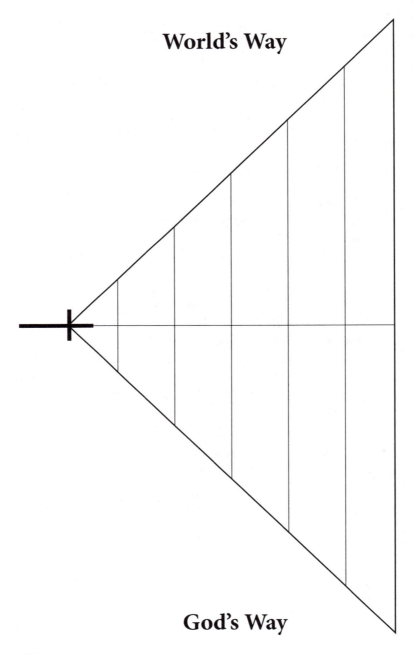

2. After completing exercise #1, study this passage
from Ephesians 2:

As for you, you were dead in your transgressions and
sins, in which you used to live when you followed the
ways of this world and of the ruler of the kingdom of the
air, the spirit who is now at work in those who are dis-
obedient. All of us also lived among them at one time,
gratifying the cravings of our sinful nature and following its desires and thoughts. Like the rest, we were by
nature objects of wrath. But because of his great love for
us, God, who is rich in mercy, made us alive with Christ
even when we were dead in transgressions—it is by
grace you have been saved. And God raised us up with
Christ and seated us with him in the heavenly realms in
Christ Jesus, in order that in the coming ages he might
show the incomparable riches of his grace, expressed in
his kindness to us in Christ Jesus. For it is by grace you
have been saved, through faith-and this not from yourselves, it is the gift of God—not by works, so that no
one can boast. For we are God's workmanship, created
in Christ Jesus to do good works, which God prepared
in advance for us to do.

—EPHESIANS 2:1–10

CHAPTER 10

If These Rocks Could Talk

THE VERY FIRST time I gave my testimony to a group of people, I used rocks to illustrate the landmark moments in my life. Every time I began describing a place where God had touched me, spoken to me, or altered my path, I dropped a stone on the table beside me. The stones were larger than my hand and were heavy enough to make an impact on the table, and the audience. By the time I was finished speaking, there was a row of rocks that lined the table.

I explained that in each of us God has left his markers or stones along the path of our lives, to remind us of what He has done. Some are large and quite noticeable. I have a few very obvious places where God has met me and those places were represented by the largest stones. But in between those times God left stones that were not as obvious to me. And inevitably, there are stones that God sees but of which I am completely unaware. Although I cannot fathom everything that God has been doing to bring me to Himself, He does see it.

> He has made everything beautiful in its time. He has also set eternity in the hearts of men; yet they cannot fathom what God has done from beginning to end.
> —ECCLESIASTES 3:11

ROCKS DO TALK

In every person's life there is a huge wall that has been built by the hand of God. It is a wall made up of huge events and tiny incidents where God has left His mark. For some, it remains a wall that acts as a barrier. They cannot get past it. They fear it. They misunderstand its purpose. Listen to Solomon, a man who had strayed from God's purpose, as he attempts to describe it:

> I am the man who has seen affliction by the rod of his wrath. He has driven me away and made me walk in darkness rather than light; indeed, he has turned his hand against me again and again, all day long. He has made my skin and my flesh grow old and has broken my bones. He has besieged me and surrounded me with bitterness and hardship. He has made me dwell in darkness like those long dead. *He has walled* me in so I cannot escape; he has weighed me down with chains. Even when I call out or cry for help, he shuts out my prayer. He has barred my way with blocks of stone; he has made my paths crooked. Like a bear lying in wait, like a lion in hiding, he dragged me from the path and mangled me and left me without help. He drew his bow and made me the target for his arrows. He pierced my heart with arrows from his quiver. I became the laughing-stock of all my people; they mock me in song all day long. He has filled me with bitter herbs and sated me with gall. He has broken my teeth with gravel; he has trampled me in the dust. I have been deprived of peace; I have forgotten what prosperity is. So I say, "My splendor is gone and all that I had hoped from the LORD." I remember my affliction and my wandering, the bitterness and the gall. I well remember them, and my soul is downcast within me. Yet this I call to mind and therefore I have hope: *Because of the LORD's great love we are not consumed, for his compassions never fail. They are new every morning; great is your faithfulness.* I say to myself, "The LORD

is my portion; therefore I will wait for him."
—LAMENTATIONS 3:1–24, AUTHOR'S EMPHASIS

Have you ever felt like King Solomon? Is there a time in your life where you were so off course from God's plan that you felt like you were bumping into walls? If this passage says anything about the nature of God, it is that no matter how far off course your own decisions take you, God's love continues to "wall" you in, not to imprison you but to protect you.

> Surely the arm of the LORD is not too short to save, nor his ear too dull to hear. But your iniquities have separated you from your God; your sins have hidden his face from you, so that he will not hear. For your hands are stained with blood, your fingers with guilt. Your lips have spoken lies, and your tongue mutters wicked things. No one calls for justice; no one pleads his case with integrity. They rely on empty arguments and speak lies; they conceive trouble and give birth to evil. They hatch the eggs of vipers and spin a spider's web. Whoever eats their eggs will die, and when one is broken, an adder is hatched. Their cobwebs are useless for clothing; they cannot cover themselves with what they make. Their deeds are evil deeds, and acts of violence are in their hands. Their feet rush into sin; they are swift to shed innocent blood. Their thoughts are evil thoughts; ruin and destruction mark their ways. The way of peace they do not know; there is no justice in their paths. They have turned them into crooked roads; no one who walks in them will know peace. So justice is far from us, and righteousness does not reach us. We look for light, but all is darkness; for brightness, but we walk in deep shadows. Like the blind we grope along the wall, feeling our way like men without eyes. At

midday we stumble as if it were twilight; among the strong, we are like the dead. We all growl like bears; we moan mournfully like doves. We look for justice, but find none; for deliverance, but it is far away. For our offenses are many in your sight, and our sins testify against us. Our offenses are ever with us, and we acknowledge our iniquities: rebellion and treachery against the LORD, turning our backs on our God, fomenting oppression and revolt, uttering lies our hearts have conceived. So justice is driven back, and righteousness stands at a distance; truth has stumbled in the streets, honesty cannot enter. Truth is nowhere to be found, and whoever shuns evil becomes a prey. The LORD looked and was displeased that there was no justice. He saw that there was no one, he was appalled that there was no one to intervene; so his own arm worked salvation for him, and his own righteousness sustained him. He put on righteousness as his breastplate, and the helmet of salvation on his head; he put on the garments of vengeance and wrapped himself in zeal as in a cloak. According to what they have done, so will he repay wrath to his enemies and retribution to his foes; he will repay the islands their due. From the west, men will fear the name of the LORD, and from the rising of the sun, they will revere his glory. For he will come like a pent-up flood that the breath of the LORD drives along. "The Redeemer will come to Zion, to those in Jacob who repent of their sins," declares the LORD. "As for me, this is my covenant with them," says the LORD. "My Spirit, who is on you, and my words that I have put in your mouth will not depart from your mouth, or from the mouths of your children, or from the mouths of their descendants from this time on and forever," says the LORD.

—Isaiah 59:1–21

But for those of us who have stopped long enough to recognize God's hand, the wall no longer looks like a barrier or something that keeps us out. Rather, we recognize God's grace in creating in us a memorial to His glory. As stated in Ecclesiastes, we cannot possibly fathom everything that God has done. You see, from our limited perspective we can only see some of the stones. There are gaps in our memories and understanding. Sometimes it looks like there are gaps in God's wall...places where He was not there. But this we can know by faith: there are *no* gaps in the wall that God has built! Every stone, every pebble, every piece of sand "cries out" the message that God has been there. Yes, even the rocks cry out. The wall of His glory in every life is higher and longer than the eye can see. It is not a barrier. Each life is a part of His temple...the place where He lives and is glorified. God Himself lives within the memory stones of our lives! Glory be to God!

> For we are God's workmanship, created in Christ Jesus to do good works, which God prepared in advance for us to do. Therefore, remember that formerly you who are Gentiles by birth and called "uncircumcised" by those who call themselves "the circumcision" (that done in the body by the hands of men)—remember that at that time you were separate from Christ, excluded from citizenship in Israel and foreigners to the covenants of the promise, without hope and without God in the world. But now in Christ Jesus you who once were far away have been brought near through the blood of Christ. For he himself is our peace, who has made the two one and has destroyed the barrier, the dividing wall of hostility, by abolishing in his flesh the law with its commandments and regulations. His purpose was to

create in himself one new man out of the two, thus making peace, and in this one body to reconcile both of them to God through the cross, by which he put to death their hostility. He came and preached peace to you who were far away and peace to those who were near. For through him we both have access to the Father by one Spirit. Consequently, you are no longer foreigners and aliens, but fellow citizens with God's people and members of God's household, built on the foundation of the apostles and prophets, with Christ Jesus himself as the chief cornerstone. In him the whole building is joined together and rises to become a holy temple in the Lord. And in him you too are being built together to become a dwelling in which God lives by his Spirit.

—EPHESIANS 2:10–22

EVERY LIFE A CULTURE

When I was in college I was assigned to read the book by Don Richardson called *Peace Child*. Actually, it was required reading for my cross-cultural communication class. If you have any curiosity about missions, that book is a must read. It is the story of how God placed His redeeming message inside the culture of a very remote and treacherous group of people. When a missionary finally reached them, the task of bringing the Gospel to a people who viewed Judas as a hero, because of his betrayal of a friend, seemed impossible. Even in such an unlikely place and culture, the "rocks cried out" and the message was eventually received.

I was so fascinated by the story that I went on to read another of Mr. Richardson's books, called *Eternity in Their Hearts*.[1] This book is not just the story of one culture where God has left His mark, but rather it relays many stories with that theme. Although all of the stories are fascinating, the opening story has had a lasting impact on me and anytime I need a little inspiration, I read the story again.

****

Five centuries before Christ, a plague broke out in Athens, Greece. As the city's council members were struggling to discover the cause of the plague, they also pondered why their numerous sacrifices to their gods had not produced any results.

It was believed, at the time, that one of the many gods they worshipped had cursed them, due to a crime of treachery committed by their King. And although they had offered sacrifices to all the gods, the plague had not lifted.

Finally one of the council members declared that there must be another god, one not familiar to them, that had caused the plague and who must be appeased. They decided to fetch a man from the island of Crete. His name was Epimenides and was considered to be very wise.

When Epimenides arrived, he marveled at the vast array of gods worshipped by the Athenians. The idols lined the streets and covered the rocky acropolis. Yet even with the large number of gods, there was still another that required their attention.

Epimenides gave his instructions to the council. The following morning they were to bring a flock of sheep, stonemasons, a large supply of stones and mortar to the grassy slope of Mars Hill. The sheep were all to be healthy and be prevented from grazing so that they would be hungry.

The council members arrived with the sheep and all other supplies the following morning as instructed. Epimenides began to speak.

> "You have expended great effort in offering sacrifice to your numerous gods, yet all has proved futile. I am about to offer sacrifices...to a god whose name

113

is unknown to us, and who is not represented by any idol in your city.

"Invoke a god whose name is unknown?" blurted an elder.

"Any god great enough and good enough to do something about the plague is probably also great enough and good enough to smile upon us in our ignorance—if we acknowledge our ignorance and call upon him!"

"Now!" called Epimenides, "...release the sheep! But let a man follow each animal and watch it closely." Then Epimenides prayed, "O thou unknown god! Reveal your willingness to respond by causing any sheep that pleases you to lie down upon the grass. And those you choose we sacrifice to you—acknowledging our pitiful ignorance of your name!"

Epimenides sat down and signaled the shepherds to step aside. Quickly, the sheep spread out across the hillside and began to graze.

"It's hopeless," a councilman muttered. "It's early morning, and I've seldom seen a flock so eager to graze. Not one will choose to rest until its belly's full, and who will then believe 'twas a god that caused it?"

"Epimenides must have chosen this time of day on purpose!" responded one of the elders. "Only thus may we know that a sheep which lies down does so by the will of this unknown god and not by its own inclination!"

One by one, sheep began to settle on the grass. Epimenides instructed the elders to mark the place where each sheep rested and let the stone masons build an altar at each spot.

One of the council members asked which god's name should be engraved on the altars, but Epimenides replied:

"Name? The Deity whose help we seek has been pleased to respond to our admission of ignorance. If now we pretend to be knowledgeable by engraving a name...I fear we shall offend Him! Inscribe the words *agnosto theo*—to an unknown god—upon the side of each altar. Nothing more is necessary."

Immediately the plague on the city began to lift and flower garlands of gratitude were draped over the humble altars on the side of Mars Hill.

****

Six hundred years later, a certain man was visiting Athens and happened to see one of those small altars along the hillside:

While Paul was waiting for them in Athens, he was greatly distressed to see that the city was full of idols. So he reasoned in the synagogue with the Jews and the God-fearing Greeks, as well as in the marketplace day by day with those who happened to be there. A group of Epicurean and Stoic philosophers began to dispute with him. Some of them asked, "What is this babbler trying to say?" Others remarked, "He seems to be advocating foreign gods." They said this because Paul was preaching the good news about Jesus and the resurrection. Then they took him and brought him to a meeting of the Areopagus, where they said to him, "May we know what this new teaching is that you are presenting? You are bringing some strange ideas to our ears, and we want to know what they mean." (All the Athenians and the foreigners who lived there spent their time doing nothing but talking about and listening to the latest ideas.) Paul then stood up in the meeting of the Areopagus and said: "Men of Athens! I see that in every way you are very religious. For as I walked around and looked carefully at your objects of worship, I even found an altar with this inscription:

> TO AN UNKNOWN GOD. *Now what you worship as something unknown I am going to proclaim to you.*
> —Acts 17:16–23, author's emphasis

Even in a land known for worshiping many idols, the true God had made Himself known and had placed a marker that would "cry out" six centuries later and provide a key to unlock the hearts and minds of the Athenians. So, why this lengthy story?

Just as God has made His mark on every human culture, He has made His mark in every human heart. It does not matter whether the mark is within a person's heritage, environment, behavior, capabilities, beliefs, or identity; the marker stone "cries out" the praise and glory of God. So many times this message is locked up, but is waiting for someone else to unlock its mystery, just like Paul unlocked the mystery of the "Unknown God" to the Athenians.

Imagine it. Every person that you meet, no matter how different from you on the outside, has a Mars Hill within them and a disheveled altar to an "unknown god." Some event has happened in their past that brought them together with God and a stone marker has been placed. They do not know what the marker means or Who it represents, but they are awaiting the time for someone to make it known to them. That is really what is meant by Ecclesiastes 3:11:

> He has made everything beautiful in its time. He has also set eternity in the hearts of men; yet they cannot fathom what God has done from beginning to end.

From beginning to end—isn't that all of the things on our own pyramid? We cannot fathom what God has been doing in our own lives all of this time. The same is true for every person. He is drawing people to Himself and is filling in all the gaps of that long and giant wall that is His temple. God is building that wall in every person, even those who have spent their entire lives worshiping all kinds of idols. In the human heart, God leaves no stones unturned!

THE "ELIJAH" STONE

Never heard of it? It is not surprising. It is a small, smooth, black stone that I have been carrying around with me since I was in junior high. I have moved eight times since acquiring that little rock, and it has made the move with me each time. I now live in a house with my husband and two daughters and the stone is still with me. It is just a rock, right? For some reason I have kept it all of these years. Whenever I see it, it evokes a very strong memory.

Remember the camp I mentioned? Every summer it was the same tradition, a tradition that I always looked forward to. After getting up early each morning and enjoying a full day of activities and lessons, the day wound down with a walk through some trees into a campfire circle. The counselors always had the bonfire roaring by the time we got there, and all of the campers would sit on benches made of logs. Someone would play the guitar and we would sing with the glow of the fire on our faces and tiny sparks rising up through the gap in the trees. Eventually, the worship time would close and we would settle in for the evening's final lesson given by one of the counselors or the camp director. It was the highlight of every day at camp.

One particular evening, however, the tradition was abandoned. Campers were required to remain in the mess hall after dinner because preparations were being made outside that we were not allowed to see. There was great anticipation by the time we were allowed to come outside, but instead of being led through the trees to the campfire circle, we were escorted to the wide gravel driveway at the edge of the camp. There was a makeshift fire pit with wood stacked high, but no fire.

Instead of the usual worship and singing time at the beginning, one of the counselors stood up and began to tell the story of Elijah and the prophets of Baal. He told it with gusto, acting out the part of Elijah mocking the prophets, while we watched silently in the darkness. Here is the story as told from *The Message* in 1 Kings 18:

> The moment Ahab saw Elijah he said, "So it's you, old troublemaker!" "It's not I who has caused trouble in Israel," said Elijah, "but you and your government—you've dumped God's ways and commands and run off after the local gods, the Baals. Here's what I want you to do: Assemble everyone in Israel at Mount Carmel. And make sure that the special pets of Jezebel, the four hundred and fifty prophets of the local gods, the Baals, and the four hundred prophets of the whore goddess Asherah, are there." So Ahab summoned everyone in Israel, particularly the prophets, to Mount Carmel. Elijah challenged the people: "How long are you going to sit on the fence? If God is the real God, follow him; if it's Baal, follow him. Make up your minds!" Nobody said a word; nobody made a move. Then Elijah said, "I'm the only prophet of God left in Israel; and there are four hundred and fifty prophets of Baal. Let the Baal prophets bring up two oxen; let them pick one, butcher it, and lay it out on an altar on firewood—but don't ignite it. I'll take the other ox, cut it up, and lay it on the wood. But neither will I light the fire. Then you pray to your gods and I'll pray to God. The god who answers with fire will prove to be, in fact, God." All the people agreed: "A good plan—do it!" Elijah

told the Baal prophets, "Choose your ox and prepare it. You go first, you're the majority. Then pray to your god, but don't light the fire." So they took the ox he had given them, prepared it for the altar, then prayed to Baal. They prayed all morning long, "O Baal, answer us!" But nothing happened—not so much as a whisper of breeze. Desperate, they jumped and stomped on the altar they had made. By noon, Elijah had started making fun of them, taunting, "Call a little louder—he is a god, after all. Maybe he's off meditating somewhere or other, or maybe he's gotten involved in a project, or maybe he's on vacation. You don't suppose he's overslept, do you, and needs to be waked up?" They prayed louder and louder, cutting themselves with swords and knives—a ritual common to them—until they were covered with blood. This went on until well past noon. They used every religious trick and strategy they knew to make something happen on the altar, but nothing happened—not so much as a whisper, not a flicker of response. Then Elijah told the people, "Enough of that—it's my turn. Gather around." And they gathered. He then put the altar back together for by now it was in ruins. Elijah took twelve stones, one for each of the tribes of Jacob, the same Jacob to whom God had said, "From now on your name is Israel." He built the stones into the altar in honor of God. Then Elijah dug a fairly wide trench around the altar. He laid firewood on the altar, cut up the ox, put it on the wood, and said, "Fill four buckets with water and drench both the ox and the firewood." Then he said, "Do it again," and they did it. Then he said, "Do it a third time," and they did it a third time. The altar was drenched and the trench was filled with water.

—1 Kings 18:17–35

What we did not know, of course, was that for this reenactment, the counselors were not pouring water on the fire pit but rather, kerosene! No wonder they decided to forego the tradition of the campfire in the trees. We might have burned down the entire county. As it was, I am fairly certain the fire marshals were not notified of this demonstration.

> When it was time for the sacrifice to be offered, Elijah the prophet came up and prayed, "O God, God of Abraham, Isaac, and Israel, make it known right now that you are God in Israel, that I am your servant, and that I'm doing what I'm doing under your orders. Answer me, God; O answer me and reveal to this people that you are God, the true God, and that you are giving these people another chance at repentance." Immediately the fire of God fell and burned up the offering, the wood, the stones, the dirt, and even the water in the trench.
> —1 KINGS 18:36–38, MSG

At that moment a huge fireball came down out of the sky and landed on the well-fueled stack of logs. It was a phenomenal display of pyrotechnics, and I'm sure the most exciting execution of a plan hatched by our counselors, ever! What we had been forbidden to see while cloistered away inside was the installation of a long wire stretched between the boy's dorm rooftop and the top of the log pile. In the dark, the wire could not be seen. Nor could the young man perched on top of the dorm roof awaiting his cue to light the kerosene-soaked ball of rags and send the "power of God" down the wire. It was amazing, and the screams and shouts of appreciation from the campers and counselors immediately followed.

> All the people saw it happen and fell on their faces in
> awed worship, exclaiming, "GOD is the true God! GOD
> is the true God!"
> —1 KINGS 18:39, MSG

The lesson of Elijah's faithfulness and boldness in the face of such opposition was clear. Whatever opposition we felt as young believers, whatever obstacle we might face in the future, we knew that our God was *bigger*! If God could overcome for Elijah, He could overcome anything that we might encounter. What a great message, and a great delivery of that message.

The fire was lit, both in the pit and in our hearts. The evening was concluded as the counselors handed each of us a small stone. Each stone had the name of Elijah written on one side, and a Scripture reference of Galatians 1:10 on the other. It is the stone that I have carried with me all of these years. I have always associated it with that night at camp and the boldness of Elijah. Here is that passage, first in the New International Version and then in *The Message*:

> Am I now trying to win the approval of men, or of God? Or am I trying to please men? If I were still trying to please men, I would not be a servant of Christ.
> —GALATIANS 1:10

> Do you think I speak this strongly in order to manipulate crowds? Or curry favor with God? Or get popular applause? If my goal was popularity, I wouldn't bother being Christ's slave.
> —GALATIANS 1:10

What a great message for a bunch of junior high campers, all trying to find their way and their identity in the world. Elijah was accused of being a troublemaker; he definitely was not popular or wanted. Elijah showed little concern for their opinions because his identity was in the power and presence of God, rather than the approval of others. This was an incredible lesson for me when I was young—the thing is, my need to embrace this lesson is no less important now than it was then. Maybe it is even more important.

LIVING BEYOND EXERCISE

1. Craft time. Make a memory stone for yourself. You can use any smooth, flat stone that is large enough to fit a Scripture reference on one side, and a name on the other. Although my "Elijah Stone" with Galatians 3:10 is a great example, you can actually use any person of the Bible that inspires you. Another example would be Moses and perhaps Ecclesiastes 3:11. The object of this exercise is to find someone that you can relate to and let the stone remind you of God's provision and presence in your life. Opaque markers work best, and your rock can be sealed easily with spray polyurethane.

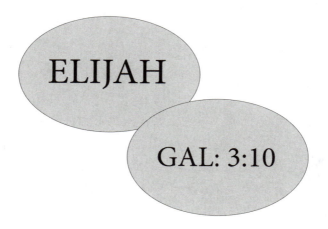

CHAPTER 11

The Pyramid Revisited: The Rest of the Story

THROUGH THIS ENTIRE series of lessons we have been focusing on the Pyramid of Change and how it affects us in relationship to how God changes us through His identity. By now we understand that our ways are not His ways and that He has the ability to change us in an instant. Our response to His change, however, is a transition that can take much longer because of our lack of ability to accept that change fully. As a result, it is sometimes difficult to see the "whole picture" of God's workmanship. Much like the picture in the first chapter, the frame we have created out of fear and self-preservation over the years often blocks our view.

In the same way, I have intentionally hidden part of the picture of the Pyramid of Change. You see, the upside-down pyramid is really only part of the story. If our own transformation was the only concern, the exchanged labels would be enough. But as described in Matthew 18, God's goal is not only to transform us, but transform others through us:

> As the Father has loved me, so have I loved you. Now remain in my love. If you obey my commands, you will remain in my love, just as I have obeyed my Father's commands and remain in his love. I have told you this so that my joy may be in you and that your joy may be complete. My command is this: Love each other as I have loved you. *Greater love has no one than this, that he lay down his life for his friends.* You are my friends

125

if you do what I command.

—John 15:9–14, author's emphasis

This is how we know what love is: Jesus Christ laid down his life for us. And we ought to lay down our lives for our brothers.

—1 John 3:16

How did Jesus "lay down" his life? His life was "poured out" for our sakes. And those that choose to follow Him are asked to do the same. Just as God has poured out His grace on us, we are called to pour out our lives for the sake of the message of reconciliation, for the sake of others! Here are a few passages from the apostle Paul's writings. Notice the connection he makes between the pouring out of God's Spirit, and the pouring out of his own life for the sake of the Gospel.

Therefore, since we have been justified through faith, we have peace with God through our Lord Jesus Christ, through whom we have gained access by faith into this grace in which we now stand. And we rejoice in the hope of the glory of God. Not only so, but we also rejoice in our sufferings, because we know that suffering produces perseverance; perseverance, character; and character, hope. And hope does not disappoint us, because God has poured out his love into our hearts by the Holy Spirit, whom he has given us.

—Romans 5:1–5

I thank Christ Jesus our Lord, who has given me strength, that he considered me faithful, appointing me to his service. Even though I was once a blasphemer and a persecutor and a violent man, I was shown mercy because I acted in ignorance and unbelief. The grace of our Lord was poured out on me abundantly, along with the faith and love that are in Christ Jesus. Here is a trustworthy saying that deserves full acceptance: Christ Jesus came into the world to save sinners-of whom I am the worst. But for that very reason I was shown mercy so that in me, the worst of sinners, Christ Jesus might display his unlimited patience as an example for those who would believe on him and receive eternal life. Now to the King eternal, immortal, invisible, the only God, be honor and glory for ever and ever. Amen.

—1 Timothy 1:12–17

For I am already being poured out like a drink offering, and the time has come for my departure. I have fought the good fight, I have finished the race, I have kept the faith. Now there is in store for me the crown of righteousness, which the Lord, the righteous Judge, will award to me on that day-and not only to me, but also to all who have longed for his appearing.

—2 Timothy 4:6–8

The Bigger Picture

Are you ready to see the bigger picture? In Chapter 2, when I first described the pyramid I explained that I did not exactly know why the flipped pyramid was so important. If you recall, I only flipped the chart's labels first and kept the pyramid pointed up rather than down. It was only months later that I realized why having the point down, at least for this illustration, was so important.

Our life in Christ is intended to affect others. There is a certain "gravity" that occurs when our life comes from His identity rather than our own. Our life in Christ is meant to be "poured out" for others, so they can hear and receive the Gospel. Rather than just an upside-down pyramid, our life seen from a larger perspective is more like the upper container of an hourglass. Can you see it?

All of who we are—our heritage, environment, behavior, capabilities, beliefs, and identity—is being poured into other people's lives, or un-flipped pyramid, *through* His identity. It is how the Gospel message passes from one generation of believers to the next.

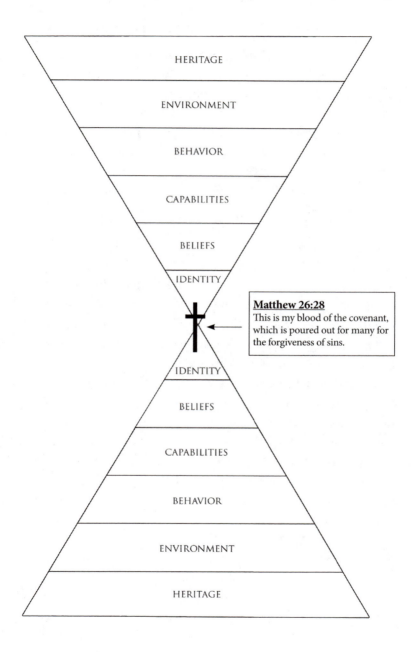

Matthew 26:28
This is my blood of the covenant, which is poured out for many for the forgiveness of sins.

Like Sands Through the Hourglass

When I was first beginning my graduate degree, a professor gave me some words of wisdom. I was pondering the cost of continuing my education, both financial costs and time away from my family. The professor said that people always found a way to come up with the money for what they really wanted to do. And as for time? He said, "The next two years are going to pass whether you pursue the degree or not!" His point was not how *much* time it would take, but rather what I did with that time.

There are really two ways in which we "spend" our lives...time and money. The time of our life will be spent regardless of *how* we spend it. One question to ask ourselves is, are we spending it by pouring it out into the lives of others, or are we spending it on embellishing our own frame? It's a tough question. It is not the size of the house, the car, or any other blessings that God chooses to lavish on us. Rather, it is how we use the house, the car, and the blessings of God.

When I was in college I had the opportunity to attend a college group that met in a church member's house. Although the house was quite large, it was crowded with young students. I could hardly fit inside the crowded living room! Although the living room was also large, the man chose not to have any furniture in his living room. Why? Because at least once a week crowds of college kids came to hear about the saving grace of Jesus Christ. The man was not young or particularly hip. He was, however, spending his life investing in the lives of all of those college kids. He had a big house, but he had an even bigger heart for God and all of those college students!

The other question, of course, is how we spend our money. Again, it is not the size of a bank account, but the availability of that gift from God to be given back to his ministry of reconciliation and be invested into the lives of others. How are we spending our money? This is not intended to be a guilt trip, but rather an honest look at what we truly value. When seen from lives where we have been transformed and live with the "point down" on our pyramid, the way we choose to spend our money should also reflect the transformation.

TIME AND MONEY

How we view ourselves, through the categories on the pyramid, can greatly affect how we spend our time and money. What we fear on that pyramid also plays a role in how we can misuse the gifts of time and money to enhance our own frame rather than live through His identity. Here are a few examples.

Let's say a person heard someone refer to him as "dumb" when he was young. Later in life, that label may still affect him, even though it is not true. The environment in which he grew up may have supported this image. To overcome the fear of that label as an adult, he may spend lots of money filling his house with books to prove how learned and well read he is. Living his life through Christ's identity, this person can be freed from the fear of that label, and freed from the habit of buying books for the sake of image.

Another example comes from our own nation's heritage. I have met several people who grew up during the Depression. Here is a quote from a woman who endured the Depression and the impact it still has on her current life when asked what she had learned:

> "*Don't waste anything.* You learn to appreciate everything you receive and try to use it to its fullest before you throw it away. You can see that by looking at my house," she says, while laughing.

Many of those who lived through the Depression have a heritage of poverty. They have learned to appreciate everything, but they also fear having nothing. Some have responded to this heritage by becoming hoarders.

Several years ago my husband and I helped his mother move out of a house that she had lived in for twenty-five years. Although she didn't have a lot of furniture, it took hours to sift through all of the little stuff that had been saved over those years. At one point I discovered a forgotten drawer with dusty spools of thread in the bottom. The spools looked like she had bought them the same year she moved into the house. There were other bits of seemingly useless items and I decided to just tip the drawer directly into a garbage can. We were moving her, after all, and from my limited point of view, she certainly would not need those spools of thread.

My mother-in-law quickly rushed over to rescue the treasures from being thrown away. You just never know when you are going to need some dusty pieces of thread. To me it was junk...but to her, a woman who had come to value the small things due to her Depression-era upbringing, those pieces of thread were worth saving!

Here is a final example: it is not uncommon for parents to experience the "empty nest" syndrome. Years of time and money poured into children are good things. But remember, being a parent is only one role that God may ask us to fulfill. If you have chosen to be a parent, it is still only part of God's picture for your life. The empty nest syndrome occurs most significantly for those who have invested in only that part of the picture. After that role is over, a person may fear that their purpose is over, as well.

One of the things that I admired most about my parents was that I was *not* the only purpose in their lives. My childhood was filled with "card parties" and bowling leagues. They weren't card parties and bowling leagues for the kids, these were the events that my parents enjoyed with other adults. Although we were present for these events, we knew that they were not intended to serve or entertain us. I used to love going around from table to table, nibbling out of the candy dishes and chatting a little with my parents' guests. Many times I would sit on the floor with my head on a couch pillow and listen to them tell their stories and burst out with laughter that filled the room.

When all of their daughters had left home for college and self-sufficiency, my parents' social life did not skip a beat. They still entertain quite a bit, play cards, play on bowling leagues, and sit around with their friends and tell stories. I asked my mom recently if she experienced the "empty nest" syndrome. She said that although she missed us, she also had so many other things to do that she didn't really feel badly about our growing up and growing out of her home. Her identity was not summed up in the role of "mother" only. She had wisely invested in many other avenues and roles in her life so that when one role changed or was removed, she was not left empty.

GODLY TREASURE

It is the pouring out of our lives into the lives of others, then, that represents the true picture and purpose of our lives. Only a life that has been turned upside-down by God can truly reflect that purpose. This is what Jesus meant when He spoke these words:

> Anyone who loves his father or mother more than me is not worthy of me; anyone who loves his son or daughter more than me is not worthy of me; and

anyone who does not take his cross and follow me is not worthy of me. Whoever finds his life will lose it, and whoever loses his life for my sake will find it.

—MATTHEW 10:37–39

LIVING BEYOND EXERCISE

1. Identify the areas of where you may be investing out of fear, rather than out of your relationship with God and His identity. Begin to pray for God's direction in these areas and let His Holy Spirit move you in a direction that serves Him and His purpose for your life.

	TIME	MONEY
IDENTITY		
BELIEFS		
CAPABILITIES		
BEHAVIOR		
ENVIRONMENT		
HERITAGE		

2. Meditate on Luke 12:13–34. What does the passage say? How does this passage speak to you in regards to your own life? When referring to the exercise above, what do you "treasure" as reflected by how you spend your time and money?

Someone in the crowd said to him, "Teacher, tell my brother to divide the inheritance with me." Jesus replied, "Man, who appointed me a judge or an arbiter between you?" Then he said to them, "Watch out! Be on your guard against all kinds of greed; a *man's life does not consist in the abundance of his possessions.*" And he told them this parable: "The ground of a certain rich man produced a good crop. He thought to himself, 'What shall I do? I have no place to store my crops.' "Then he said, 'This is what I'll do. I will tear down my barns and build bigger ones, and there I will store all my grain and my goods. And I'll say to myself, "You have plenty of good things laid up for many years. Take life easy; eat, drink and be merry."' "But God said to him, 'You fool! This very night your life will be demanded from you. Then who will get what you have prepared for yourself?' *"This is how it will be with anyone who stores up things for himself but is not rich toward God.*" Then Jesus said to his disciples: "Therefore I tell you, do not worry about your life, what you will eat; or about your body, what you will wear. Life is more than food, and the body more than clothes. Consider the ravens: They do not sow or reap, they have no storeroom or barn; yet God feeds them. And *how much more valuable you are than birds!* Who of you by worrying can add a single hour to his life? Since you cannot do this very little thing, why do you worry about the rest? "Consider how the lilies grow. They do not labor or spin. Yet I tell you, not even Solomon in all his splendor was dressed like one of these. If that is how God clothes the grass of the field, which is here today, and tomorrow is thrown into the fire, how much more will he clothe you, O you of little faith! And do not set your heart on what you will eat or drink; do not worry about it. For the pagan world runs after all such things, and your Father knows that you need them. *But seek his kingdom, and these things will be given to you as well.* "Do not be afraid, little flock, for your Father has been pleased to give you the kingdom. Sell your possessions and give to the poor. Provide purses for yourselves that will not wear out, a treasure in heaven that will not be exhausted, where no thief comes near and no moth destroys. For *where your treasure is, there your heart will be also.*

—LUKE 12:13–34, AUTHOR'S EMPHASIS

CHAPTER 12

Lessons From the Frame

AFTER SO MUCH time spent looking at God's workmanship, it is finally time to return to the frame. Please note that this study is not called *Breaking the Frame* or *Busting Out of the Frame.* The frame has value and is part of God's plan in His purpose for our lives. A life's frame, in the right proportion and without our embellishment, is a gift from God and provides the necessary structure for the masterpiece of His workmanship to bring glory to Him.

Several years ago my husband and I were attending a missionary and pastor's conference in Sydney, Australia. Early one morning, Harlan took a long walk and had a unique experience talking with God among the unfamiliar trees, flowers, and wildlife. When he returned later, I could tell that something had changed. He had been with God in a special way. He tried to describe the setting and the experience as he attempted to share the joy and words he had received.

At the end of the trip, Harlan and I were passing an art gallery when he stopped in his tracks. He pointed to a signed watercolor print and said, "That's it. That was where I was when I was with God." Well, the picture was beautiful and serene. No wonder he had a difficult time describing his surroundings. The textures and plants and smells were all so unfamiliar and distinct to the Australian landscape.

I knew immediately that I wanted to go back and purchase that print. I made up a reason to get away from Harlan just long enough to find my way back to the gallery. The print was not framed, but came in one of those long protective tubes. To avoid being conspicuous, I gave the tube to one of our fellow conference attendees for safekeeping and travel back to the States. Two months later I was able to surprise my husband with the print, still unframed, for Christmas. My hope for him was that the print would always remind him of the special time that he had experienced with God, hearing His voice, hearing His call on his life. I hoped that it would act as a stone of remembrance for him.

That should be the end of the story, right? Well, unfortunately, that beautiful picture stayed inside its tube for nearly four years. As anyone who has bought a relatively inexpensive print and attempted to have it custom-framed will tell you, the framing can be much more expensive than the art. Because of its size and shape, the frame would cost approximately three times as much as the artwork. Well, we just could not bring ourselves to spend that much money.

Finally, just before Christmas 2004, I found a framer who would accomplish the task for one third of the original framing quotation. I felt a little embarrassed about giving my husband nearly the same gift for Christmas again. By this time, I didn't know if the picture held the same depth of meaning it once had.

Harlan's response after opening the present reminded me again of how impacting those meetings with God can be. Harlan immediately hung the newly matted and framed print on the wall across from our bed, so that when he sits up every morning, it is the first thing he sees. To say that the picture is in a prominent and personal place is an understatement. We have been living in our house for four years and still have pictures in boxes and inside closets, waiting to be hung. Harlan was hanging that picture while the rest of us were still down-stairs opening presents.

So what did the frame do for the picture? What does a frame provide that the picture lacks without it?

ENHANCES THE ART

Well, there is no question that the biggest enhancement for Harlan's picture was the ability to actually view the picture. In four years the print was probably only removed from its tube a few times. If you want to enjoy a work of art, the art needs to be displayed. Obviously, the frame provides for that possibility. The frame, in proper proportion and style, brings appreciation for the art and glory to the artist.

"We are His workmanship, created for..."(Eph. 2:10). It is not difficult to see the spiritual lesson in God's work needing God's frame. If our lives are hidden in a tube, our lives cannot bring glory to Him who created us. Through God-given roles, responsibilities, gifts, talents, and our obe-dience, our life can be displayed to others for His glory. That is God's will for your life.

> You are the light of the world. A city on a hill cannot be hidden. Neither do people light a lamp and put it under a bowl. Instead they put it on its stand, and it gives light to everyone in the house.
> —MATTHEW 5:14–15

Verse 15 could be paraphrased to read, "Neither do people purchase a work of art and hide it in a tube. Instead they put it in its frame, and it gives inspiration to everyone in the house." *You* are that light, that city, that lamp, that work of art.

STRUCTURE

I have a friend who used to be in the framing business (of course, where was she when I needed Harlan's picture framed?) and she gave a little demonstration to one of my classes of how a frame is constructed.

As a framer, the most important part of the job is to preserve the artwork. It can easily get dirty, wrinkled, torn, or even misplaced. When constructing the frame, the measurement must be 100 percent accurate. The slightest error when cutting the molding can result in a weak frame that will risk the integrity and preservation of the art.

The frame is made of four pieces that are joined together in a mitered cut. After cutting the four pieces of the frame, the framer must glue the edges and join them together with a special joint nail machine. All of the strength from the joining nails is from the back of the frame, usually unseen from the front. The seam between each piece of wood must not have any gaps or again, the frame is weakened.

Sometimes, when the frame is large and cumbersome it requires two people to join the wood together. One person cannot accomplish the framing task alone because it is too difficult to keep the seams square during the nailing process. My friend explained that on several occasions she had attempted to create a large frame without anyone's help and the results were disastrous.

God provides our lives with structure and in most cases that structure requires more than just us to hold it together and remain strong. Think of all the people in your life that "hold you together" during times of stress. Think of all those roles you fulfill that keep you "in place." And how many of those roles also serve to keep others in place? God's appointed structure to our lives is imperative to our growth and the growth of others. Those roles and responsibilities are not traps or prisons, but rather they are part of the God-given support and structure from which He can be glorified:

> They devoted themselves to the apostles' teaching and to the fellowship, to the breaking of bread and to prayer. Everyone was filled with awe, and many wonders and miraculous signs were done by the apostles. All the believers were together and had everything in common. Selling their possessions and goods, they gave to anyone as he had need. Every day they continued to meet together in the temple courts. They broke bread in their homes and ate together with glad and sincere hearts, praising God and enjoying the favor of all the people. And the Lord added to their number daily those who were being saved.
>
> —ACTS 2:42–47

PROTECTION

Light

Very important (and usually expensive) pieces of art are now framed under UV protective glass. Colors can fade over time when exposed to certain kinds of light if not properly protected. And of course, faded colors lessen the beauty of the original artwork and decrease its value.

Humidity and warping

When I was attempting to get the picture framed for my husband, the framer asked me where the picture would eventually be hung. I was curious why he had asked. He explained that if the artwork were to be displayed where there was moisture, like in a bathroom, the art would need to be mounted on a different surface to protect it from warping. Warping devalues the art, and contributes to eventual destruction.

Dust and vermin

If I had left my husband's picture in that storage tube for many more years, it is likely that the integrity of the art would have been compromised. The tube was perfect for short-term storage, but it was not intended to protect the art for any great length of time. Eventually dust, dirt, and possibly bugs would have breached the barrier and the art would have suffered deterioration. When a picture is properly framed, the art is sealed within, which prevents dust and vermin to compromise it.

Theft

The following story illustrates how a frame serves as protection from theft.

> On August 21, 1911, the world's most famous work of art—Leonardo da Vinci's *Mona Lisa*—was stolen from the Louvre museum in Paris. That morning, many museum employees noticed that the painting was not hanging in its usual place, but they assumed the painting was taken off the wall by the museum photographer who was shooting pictures of it in his studio.
>
> By Tuesday morning, when the painting had not been returned and it was not in the photographer's studio, museum officials were notified. The painting was gone!
>
> The police immediately were contacted and they set up headquarters in the museum curator's office. The entire museum, a forty-nine acre building, was searched from top to bottom for an entire week. The only thing a detective found was the heavy frame that once held the Mona Lisa. It was discovered in a staircase leading to a cloakroom.
>
> Luckily, the painting was recovered twenty-seven months after it was stolen. An Italian man named Vincenzo Perugia claimed he stole the work out of

patriotism. He did not think such a work by a famous Italian should be kept in France.

How did Perugia steal the Mona Lisa? He had spent Sunday night in the Louvre, hiding in an obscure little room. Monday morning, while the museum was closed, he entered the room where the painting was kept and unhooked it from the wall. In a staircase, he cut the painting from its frame. He then walked out of the Louvre and into the pages of history.

Notice that the first thing the thief did was to cut the Mona Lisa out of its frame. Why? Because a painting is harder to steal when the frame is on. In spiritual terms, there is one who is always trying to steal us away from God, but we all belong to God. His frame and presence makes us more difficult to steal.

> Therefore Jesus said again, "I tell you the truth, I am the gate for the sheep. All who ever came before me were thieves and robbers, but the sheep did not listen to them. I am the gate; whoever enters through me will be saved. He will come in and go out, and find pasture. The thief comes only to steal and kill and destroy; I have come that they may have life, and have it to the full."
>
> —JOHN 10:7–10

The frame, provided by God, does not need to be thrown away so that we can have life. The fullest life can only be experienced when we are safe from theft and living within that frame. There is freedom *and* security within it. When we choose to throw away God's framing of our lives, we open ourselves up for destruction. The boundaries have disappeared. Our protection is gone. It is only a matter of time before we are stolen away from the One who loves us most.

What Happens When You Ignore the Frame?

The *Mona Lisa's* frame was disintegrating, although much had been attempted to preserve the art. The frame was actually beginning to harm the artwork and had to be replaced. The problem was that for years all of the preservation efforts were conducted on the masterpiece itself, while the frame went relatively ignored.

The lesson, of course, is that although the artwork is the masterpiece, the frame must also be preserved. Without a strong, proportionate frame the art loses some of its beauty, its structure, and its protection. The frame of our lives should be the perfect fit that God intended so that His work of art can be everything that He intended.

> And God raised us up with Christ and seated us with him in the heavenly realms in Christ Jesus, in order that in the coming ages he might show the incomparable riches of his grace, expressed in his kindness to us in Christ Jesus. For it is by grace you have been saved, through faith—and this not from yourselves, it is the gift of God—not by works, so that no one can boast. For we are God's workmanship, created in Christ Jesus to do good works, which God prepared in advance for us to do.
>
> —Ephesians 2:6–10

Review

At the beginning of the study we discussed how labels, roles, and expectations can draw us away from God's intention for His works of art. Those roles, although important and good, can become the focus of our identity, rather than our relationship with God and His purpose for our lives.

146

For ten chapters I have sought to carefully remove the frame and take an honest look at what lies behind those roles and responsibilities. Here is a summary of what has been revealed.

The "Pyramid of Change" demonstrates how people naturally experience change. Like learning a language or breaking a habit, people are prone to move up through the pyramid from heritage, environment, behavior, capabilities, and beliefs, in an attempt to discover a new identity. This process sometimes can be very difficult and many fail to truly change their identities in the process.

Although the original pyramid of change is normal in our human nature, an altered life in Christ, rather than flowing out of a new environment, should flow from a change in identity...namely, our identity of Christ. God "flips the chart" and says to us *Not so with Me!*

Even though God has flipped the pyramid over and gives us a new identity from which to live, we still find it difficult to live our lives that way. We feel that God has given a particular vision or mission for our lives, but experience frustration at the seeming lack of progress toward that God-given picture. We feel stuck within the borders of our life's frame—lack of education or ability, familial and financial obligations, or a feeling of disqualification because we know our own weaknesses. We fear moving beyond that frame.

We discussed how *fear* (or: false, evidence, appearing, real) could immobilize us. We reviewed the story about a traveler who could not progress on his journey because of a bull in the middle of the road, but soon discovered that many times the very thing we fear is the thing that, if confronted, will propel us toward our greatest success for the Lord.

Whatever we fear causes us to check every move, question

every decision, and can spiritually immobilizes us. The problem, however, is every correction attempted distracts us from God's purpose. Remember the story about the boating excursion and the affect of speed on overcorrection? God can correct our path even while we are moving on it.

We reviewed the Wheel of Life and discovered that regardless of our current age, each of us has only a limited amount of time. It is difficult to bring goods news of being new to another person without first experiencing its reality in ourselves. Whatever fears held us back prior to God reconciling us, we must now move beyond them and beyond the constraints of the original pyramid.

Much time was spent on the life of Moses. If anyone had a reason to fear he was disqualified by his past, it was Moses. Yet the calling of God was the qualification from God—and so it is with all whom God calls.

We reviewed the attitudes of the Israelites during the Exodus and reviewed their list of complaints against God and Moses. We discussed how often human nature drives us to desire slavery rather than risk freedom in the unknown places that God may lead.

We discovered that although the people complained, God endured them and was prepared to deliver the Promised Land to them after only two years in the desert. Unfortunately, it was not the complaining or worshiping an idol that kept them from the land, it was the sin of fear.

The purpose of the forty years in the desert was to rid the people of their fear and pride. In that scenario, it required the passing of a generation, but God leads us through our own "wilderness" to accomplish the same thing.

After reviewing the desert journey through the Israelites perspective, we reviewed it specifically through Moses' own transformation from sheepherder to the confident confronter of Pharaoh, to the pastor of a nation. The transformation was only possible because he spent time with God and moved beyond the fear into obedience.

We finally took one more glimpse at the people who would not inherit the land and attempted to experience the amazing regret as a result of their fear and pride. They missed their purpose. We discussed the impact of "the race not run." God calls us to run, not just rehearse. Running, then, is living beyond the frame.

When it was finally time to capture the land God had promised, the last words of Moses to the Israelites were to remember what God had done. The words of remembering are life! Before we grasp the taking and the keeping of God's promises, we must remember what He has done.

We learned that when Joshua led the Israelites to battle, they crossed the Jordan and picked up stones from the dry riverbed to help them remember the event. Stones were commonplace there, and so are the memory markers left in our path to draw us toward God. God makes His presence known in what is most available! Even people.

It is what we remember about God's presence in our own lives that becomes the redeeming message for others. His stones are our testimonies. Whether those memories are good or bad for us makes no difference to God, because He has redeemed them all for His purpose. Even the ugly stones are part of God's workmanship and should no longer cause us shame in His identity.

We enlarged the frame of the pyramid to show how God pours out our life experiences into another's life. The upside-down pyramid, or a life lived with God's identity as the source, becomes the top container of an hourglass pouring its sand into the container at the bottom. A heart made ready by God, hearing the message of our life's stones, receives God and has their life turned upside down. The process begins again for a new believer.

LIVING BEYOND EXERCISE

Remember the picture in Chapter 1? Here is another picture with too large a frame. Attempt to describe the whole picture using this part as a reference:

Do you want to see what is revealed when the frame of this picture is back to an appropriate size?

Now, how observant are you? Does this picture look familiar? If you return to the picture in the very first chapter, you will notice that it is the same picture, but from a different perspective. You might have guessed, when looking at the picture in Chapter 1 that it was a beautiful beach scene. Were your perceptions the same when all you could see was the jagged rock?

Our life in God's perspective, the whole picture as it is revealed to us by Him, is the true and beautiful message that will reconcile others to Him. He supplies the frame and determines its size and we are not to embellish or enlarge it. To embellish the frame is to block out a portion of what God intended.

For some the enlarged frame might look like the exercise in Chapter 1 where all that is revealed is the beautiful water. All that is ugly or negative is carefully hidden under a large frame of stained-glass religion and the "picture" of a perfect lifestyle. Such an oversized frame is difficult to maintain and hides God's glory of the whole picture. Why would God need to redeem such a perfect life?

For others the enlarged frame may look more like the exercise in this chapter, where the only portion in view is jagged and ugly. A person maintaining this frame can often seem like a victim to all of their circumstances. It is difficult to see any joy in this type of life, and certainly difficult for God to reach others through it.

Although one large frame only shows beauty and the other only what is negative, neither frame is in proper proportion. Neither life is particularly attractive because there is beauty only in the whole picture that God has created. Although there may be ugly parts in your life, God redeems those parts for the sake of His glory and His message of reconciliation to others. And where there is beauty, God humbles us so that His whole masterpiece can be seen. Truly, God's purpose is to find us "living beyond the frame."

Notes

Chapter 6
Fear and the Wilderness Journey

1. There is much debate about how many years the Israelites were actually enslaved by the Egyptians. There are calculations, based on numerous Scripture references and Jewish tradition that place it anytime between two hundred and four hundred years. Regardless of how many years, it is obvious that by the time of the Exodus, the Israelites viewed themselves more readily as slaves than as the children of God.
2. William Bridges' materials can be found at http://www.wmbridges.com/resources.

Chapter 8
Regret and Remembrance

1. Jim Lovell, *Lost Moon: The Perilous Voyage of Apollo 13* (Boston, MA: Houghton Mifflin, 1994).
2. Web site: www.ohstrack.com/officiating.asp, accessed March 2, 2005.

Chapter 10
If These Rocks Could Talk

1. Don Richardson, *Eternity in Their Hearts* (Ventura, CA: Regal Books, 1981).

Chapter 11
The Pyramid Revisited

1. Web site: www.mcsc.k12.in.us/mhs/social/madedo/oralhist/davis1.htm, accessed May 30, 1999.

Chapter 12
Lessons From the Frame

1. Milton Esterow, *The Art Stealers* (New York: Macmillan Company, 1966).

To Contact the Author

E-mail: cheryljharris@hotmail.com